D1055230

Mark Victor Hansen

the
Infinite
Asset

the
Infinite
Asset

managing
brands
to build
new value

Sam Hill
Chris Lederer

HARVARD BUSINESS SCHOOL PRESS
BOSTON, MASSACHUSETTS

Copyright 2001 Harvard Business School Publishing Corporation

All rights reserved

Printed in the United States of America

05 04 03 02 01   5 4 3 2 1

The following names are protected through trademark laws by 3M.
3M,™ Scotch-Brite,™ O-Cel-O,™ Post-it,® Scotchgard,™ Scotch,® and
Thinsulate.™

Library of Congress Cataloging-in-Publication Data

Hill, Sam.
    The infinite asset : managing brands to build new value / Sam Hill,
Chris Lederer.
        p. cm.
    Includes bibliographical references and index.
    ISBN 1-57851-249-2
    1. Brand name products—Management. 2. Brand name products—
Management—Case studies. I. Lederer, Chris, 1965– II. Title.

HD69.B7 H55 2001
658.8'27—dc21   2001024054

The paper used in this publication meets the requirements of the American National Standard for Permanence of Paper for Publications and
Documents in Libraries and Archives Z39.48-1992.

To Liz, Rachel, and Michael—Sam
To my three E's: Elise, Emma, and Ella—Chris

contents

foreword

Kevin Lane Keller

I N RECENT YEARS, branding has become a strategic imperative, and we can often trace the success or failure of firms back to their ability or inability to build, sustain, and enhance value in their brands. Accordingly, many have written about how best to manage brands so that they reach their full potential. Nevertheless, we still have much to learn about inspiring and guiding those efforts. Hill and Lederer's book *The Infinite Asset* represents a very important step in that direction. To appreciate their contribution, we must step back and consider the most pressing brand management priorities that firms face in their pursuit of brand value maximization.

To improve profitability, we badly need greater insight into five areas of brand management.

First, marketers must blend top-down and bottom-up brand management activities more effectively. Top-down or more "macro" perspectives involve such "big picture" activities as defining brand hierarchies, assembling brand portfolios, and providing brand leadership within the firm. Bottom-up or more "micro" perspectives include such activities as achieving deep understanding with consumers or organizations, building resonance with customers, and promoting brand innovation.

Second, marketers—and organizations—must develop and embrace brand manifestos that inform and rally the entire organization around one of their most valuable assets: their brands. For example, companies can formulate brand charters—essentially, short documents that summarize critical brand-related information such as the history and importance of the brand to the firm, the values and essence of the brand and its positioning, and general guidelines for how marketers should treat the brand. Brand charters help organizations to codify brand philosophy, capture brand learnings from brand audits and other research projects, provide long-term strategic brand direction, and supply short-term tactical brand guidelines.

Third, marketers must shrewdly leverage brand partnerships and appropriately borrow equity from other entities—other brands, well-known people, places, and so on. This leveraging will involve, for example, knowing when the brand needs its image reinforced rather than augmented, and how equity transfers from these various other types of entities to the brand. Fourth, marketers must integrate their brand marketing to create bountiful synergies: by mixing and matching various brand communication and distribution options. To do so, marketers must balance considerations such as coverage and cost, uniformity and personalization, commonality and complimentarity, to maximize the collective contribution of their marketing programs.

Finally, marketers must develop brand metrics that can put all of these activities in context and—most important—allow marketers to trace how their marketing investments directly create brand value.

Remarkably, *The Infinite Asset* manages to address virtually all of these issues, and provides important insights in the process. The basic premise of the book is simple yet powerful—we create brand value, in part, through combinations with other brands where these other brands can come in all forms and from all sources. Maximizing the value of brands thus involves brand portfolio management—combining brands of all kinds from both inside and outside the firm to create brand value. Hill and Lederer persuasively argue that brand value depends on explicit *and* implicit brand partners. In other words, a brand's value depends on the company it keeps with other brands—where it's sold, what it's sold with, what brands comprise its key ingredients, and so on. This expansive view of brand management breaks new ground and correctly reflects modern marketing practices, and an increasingly networked economy. Simply put, all kinds of other brands can affect equity, a fact that most models and approaches to brand equity fail to appreciate or address.

Taking a customer perspective, Hill and Lederer provide a clever new conceptualization of brand portfolios, as well as a detailed set of tools and insights to assist brand owners in managing their portfolio. The centerpiece of their theory is the brand portfolio "molecule"—a fascinating model that represents all the elements of a brand and how they interact to create brand value. The authors supplement this concept with a fully articulated brand portfolio toolkit that addresses how to assemble a strategic vision for the brand. The toolkit provides valuable guidance for specific tactical concerns in eight areas (extensions, repositioning, pruning, over-branding, co-branding, amalgamation, partitioning, and scaling.) To enhance further the power and applicability of their ideas, they also offer direction as to the proper organizational design toward successful brand portfolio management.

The Infinite Asset contains useful examples, including in-depth case studies of 3M, Cadillac, Miller Beer, and Yahoo!. Through fresh ideas, keen insights, and rich applications Hill and Lederer deftly make progress on the difficult branding challenges that today's organizations face. Innovative and practical, *The Infinite Asset* offers well-reasoned advice with a host of benefits. In particular, adhering to their principles will help firms to address the five major branding imperatives noted above: the optimal execution of top-down brand management, the development of timeless and timely brand charters, the proper leverage of equity from other brand entities, the design of well-integrated marketing programs, and the use of informative brand metrics to trace brand value. This book is an important step in the evolution of our thinking about brands. It is creative but well grounded in the realities and challenges involved in maximizing brand value in the twenty-first century. It should stimulate thinking and provoke action and, in that sense, itself offers infinite value.

the
Infinite
Asset

understanding the
brand
portfolio

1

brands, new value creation, and competitive advantage

How queer everything is today! And yesterday things went on just as usual. I wonder if I've been changed in the light? Let me think: was I the same when I got up this morning? I almost think I can remember feeling a little different.
—Lewis Carroll, *Alice in Wonderland*

TIME WAS, brands succeeded or failed based on their own merits—the quality of the products or services they represented, their positioning in the marketplace, the appeal of their advertising campaigns. Not long ago, managing an individual brand successfully—understanding its market intricacies, engaging consumers, creating sustainable value, and increasing profitability—sufficed.

Those were the days.

Today—and this is no news flash—the bar is higher. Yes, plenty of stand-alone brands are thriving out there. And, of course, we readily acknowledge that successfully building value for a stand-alone brand still isn't a piece of cake. But the most important brand work being done today is about much more than individual brands.

Increasingly, companies are creating brand value by combining brands in new and compelling ways. Consider Volkswagen (VW) and Trek, for example, which have teamed up to sell cars and bicycles together. American Airlines, Citibank, and Visa jointly offer a credit card. Publisher Gruner + Jahr is relaunching *McCall's* as *Rosie's McCall's,* as in Rosie O'Donnell. Philips and Levi Strauss just announced a jacket with built-in electronics—a cell phone hidden in the collar and an MP3 player in one of the pockets.

Consider, too, the marketing director of the iPaq line of Internet appliances. He spends most of his day not with his agencies or his brand team, but with managers of other brands both inside and outside his parent company, Compaq. One such relationship is with Microsoft. Technically, Microsoft is iPaq's software provider. In practice, Microsoft is iPaq's marketing partner, and iPaq's marketing director discusses everything from brand identity to naming and co-badging with his counterpart at Microsoft. Recently, he made the complex strategic and financial decision to use the Microsoft PocketPC brand on every Compaq personal digital assistant (PDA).

Nor is Microsoft iPaq's only partner. The iPaq team is developing wireless e-mail devices with Blackberry, a brand for Research In Motion (RIM) in Canada. The marketing director just signed a long-term deal with America Online (AOL) to allow AOL members to access their e-mail via the iPaq Blackberry. A long list of offerings that will bear the Compaq and iPaq brands is in development, and iPaq's marketing director is involved at some level in each project.

What's more, just down the hall from his office, a separate team is selling the iPaq Internet computer. Across a red fiberglass bridge, in an adjacent building, other teams are using the Compaq brand to market everything from laptops to the business servers added to the mix when Compaq acquired Digital and Tandem. Another group is working on the Compaq corporate brand. And scores of potential new partners contact the parent company each month to pitch a joint brand venture of some kind.

What does all this mean? Put simply, it means that we are finally beginning to understand—and tap into—the true potential of brands. It means that, properly used, brands can become infinite assets, used over and over to create new value.

It means that we have moved well beyond Philip Kotler's definition of a brand as, "a name, term, sign, symbol or design, or any combination of them which is intended to identify the goods and services of one seller or group of sellers and to differentiate them from those of competitors."[1] We've also moved beyond the more current definitions of brand as the reputation that a brand builds over time (its "trustmark"), or culture, or corporate identity.

Although some of today's most exciting companies—Starbucks, Disney, and Nike for example, consider a brand to be the total experience associated with the purchase and the role of the product in the lifestyle of the user, even that view falls short of capturing the true potential of brand work in today's market.

In fact, the greatest brand value is now being created *in the intersections between individual brands.* Kmart and Martha Stewart are worth more together than they are apart. Apple is the strongest single brand proposition in the personal computer category, but the combined brand of Intel, Microsoft, and Compaq is more valuable. Branson, Missouri, has become a tourist destination to rival Las Vegas because it offers visitors the combined brands of dozens of top entertainers, such as Andy Williams and Yakhov Smirnoff.

The downside? If we can create value in the space between brands, then we can destroy it as well. The market can reject the combination, partners can disagree over direction, brands can even contaminate each other. Look at what happened to the brands in the Audi line, after the Audi 5000's problems.

Audi owners first began to report an unusually high rate of sudden acceleration cases in 1986. Cars accelerated by themselves, either rear-ending vehicles in front of them or crashing through garage walls. The television program *60 Minutes* ran a story in November of that year. A wave of publicity and a federal study followed, and Audi 5000 sales plummeted.

Mary Sullivan, of the University of Chicago, studied the case in 1990. She eschewed anecdotal evidence and qualitative consumer research and studied impacts in terms of real dollars, measuring the financial effects of this publicity on the 5000s, and on other Audi brands. She rigorously accounted for advertising and competitive activities in evaluating the effects of the incident on the depreciation rate of the Audi 5000, as well as the effects on the Audi 4000 and the Quattro. And she concluded that, over the two years following the broadcast, the controversy caused the 5000's value to depreciate 7 percent to 12 percent faster than it would have otherwise. More important, other models with no such problems all fared similarly. The Audi 4000 depreciated 8.4 percent to 11 percent more than it should have, and the Quattro suffered a 6.1 percent penalty. Sullivan believes the Audi 4000 took a greater hit than the Quattro because the 4000's positioning is so close to that of the 5000.

Audi is an obvious example because all the brands exist under a single umbrella, but the danger is really no less for brands with less explicit and deliberate links. In the year 2000, many car companies struggled to overcome the negative brand halo cast by the Firestone tire recall. Harvard University is in the headlines because Forum Financial is suing it over consulting work performed by a former professor.[2] Every brand manager now lives with the reality that another brand manager in a completely different brand area can affect his brand in important, unexpected ways.

We believe managers can leverage the potential power among brands and minimize the risk simultaneously. The answer lies in managing brands as portfolios and, more important, *in updating and rethinking the traditional view of what a brand portfolio is and how it works.*

This Is Not Your Father's Brand Portfolio

Ours is not the first proposal for managing brands as systems. In the late 1980s, Procter & Gamble (P&G) instituted category management, creating general managers to oversee groups of brands in the same category. In 1992, Jean-Noel Kapferer proposed his hierarchy of brands, with six levels of brands including product brands, line brands, and umbrella brands—an extraordinary insight. In 1996, David Aaker constructed an innovative framework for thinking about brand systems and characterized brand roles as "drivers," "endorsers," "fighter brands," and "silver bullets."

Our work builds on these ideas but differs in three critical ways.

1. Our definition of brand portfolio does not restrict membership to brands owned by one company. (For discussion, we'll call that type of grouping a "brand system." A brand system, in other words, would contain only the brands that a single company owns and uses together, for example, Hewlett-Packard (HP) and LaserJet.)

   Our brand portfolio, on the contrary, includes *every* brand that plays in the consumer's decision to buy. Intel drives Dell's new product strategy. Dell marketers should consider Intel part of Dell's brand portfolio. The price of a Hertz rental car depends on whether the customer flew United or American. Hertz marketers should consider the airlines part of the Hertz portfolio, since they clearly drive both choice and pricing. The National Basketball Association's (NBA) marketing plan depends on its contracts with Nike, NBC, TNT, and so forth.

   On the other hand, *not* every brand the company owns should be in the portfolio. Does the buyer of a Kohler faucet care about Kohler's string of golf resorts? Probably not.[3]

2. Traditional brand system mapping doesn't work for brand portfolios as we define them. Aaker says brand systems "fall into a natural hierarchy."[4] For example, in a brand system hierarchy, Philip Morris naturally sits over its divisional brands—Miller, Kraft, Marlboro, et al. Kraft is over Maxwell House, Jell-O, Philadelphia Cream Cheese, and right on down the line. Traditional hierarchies neatly capture most of the brands in a given company on one page and reflect the brand organization—the reporting relationships of the brand managers—from the inside.

   To manage our brand portfolios, on the other hand, we must consider the consumer's point of view as well. That is, we should know how important each brand is in the consumer's purchase decision. For a Marlboro purchaser, for example, the Philip Morris brand matters very little. And so, in a portfolio created for Marlboro, Philip Morris should go at the bottom of the page, not the top. Would the Philip Morris name always be at the bottom? Not necessarily. That's another difference with our brand portfolios: they're dynamic.

3. Finally, in our approach, the traditional brand organization doesn't suffice. More traditional "brand systems" focus on managing a single brand. Even when a company employs category management, as Kevin Lane Keller says, "the duties of the individual brand managers, however, [are] essentially unchanged."[5] That is, brand managers go all out to build their individual brands, and category managers coordinate their actions after the fact. We must manage brands individually, to be sure; but to create new value, that's not enough. In our view, brand portfolio management is active, preemptive, and overarching. Brand portfolio managers are strategic activists, who help set and oversee the brand agenda inside and beyond a firm's own brand system.

The Brand Value Frontier

Consider this analogy (it's not perfect, but it serves our purpose well). A mutual fund manager creates his fund by selecting stocks according to the overall goal of the fund and each stock's expected risk and return. Some managers focus on an industry sector, a geographical region, growth, value, or some other element. The stocks in the fund are diverse and separate. Individually, no stock meets the overarching fund goals. Collectively— that is, as combinations of stocks with different levels of risk and return—they do. A portfolio of stocks typically has relatively lower risk for its expected return. By managing the stocks as a portfolio rather than as individual equities, the manager has presumably optimized value. Similarly, managing brand portfolios is key to maximizing brand returns.

In five years, we believe, the most forward-thinking companies will value and manage brand portfolios just they do financial portfolios today. Brand portfolio strategists will search for the efficient frontier of the brand set, the boundary where brand managers can maximize their returns for any level of portfolio risk, much as savvy investors do today. Instead of the sales and shares of individual brands, they will discuss objectives like overall portfolio growth rate and minimizing risk by adding or removing new brands.

In ten years, we will see brand-based business models become the dominant corporate life form. Scott Bedbury, senior vice president of marketing at Starbucks, already calls brand the "central organizing principle of a company."[6] The successful twenty-first-century corporation will not be a collection of buildings, equipment, and products, but a collection of brands and the activities that support them. In short, brands will exceed marketing.

To make this leap, we must first understand the basics of brand portfolio management.

2

elements of the new model

The significant problems we face cannot be solved at the same level of thinking we were at when we created them.
   —Widely attributed to Albert Einstein

To SUCCESSFULLY MANAGE a brand portfolio, a company needs three things: a true visualization, or graphic representation, of the entire portfolio depicting all the brands, their characteristics, and the relationships among them and to the outside world; a set of tools with which to manage the brand portfolio; and an organization designed with this new approach in mind.

Visualizing the Portfolio

The most successful brand portfolio managers will use a dynamic, quantitatively driven map of the entire portfolio. We call this map a "molecule," because that is what it looks like.

FIGURE 2-1

Brand Portfolio Molecule: Cadillac, 2000

Steinmetz-Opel

Catera
DHS
DTS

DeVille

Caddie
Seville
STS
Evoq
Le Mans Racing
SLS

Escalade

Team Cadillac

Pebble Beach
Senior PGA Tour

EWGA

PGA

Allante
Elvis Presley

Fleetwood
Cimarron
Potamkin (etc.)

Eldorado

Bose
Michelin
Cadillac
Bosch
Magnasteer
StabiliTrak
OnStar
Toyota
Northstar

Twilight Sentinel

Night Vision
Zebrano wood
General Motors
PASS-Key II

Figure 2-1 is a Brand Portfolio Molecule (BPM) for Cadillac. In sum, it captures five dimensions of information: the brands that are relevant to purchasers, the importance of those brands, the influence of those brands, the relationship between those brands, and the ability of management to control those brands. See chapter 3 for a detailed discussion of the molecule.

We are going to devote chapter 3 to constructing a "brand portfolio molecule" (BPM) such as the one shown in figure 2-1. But we'll describe it in broad strokes here. Building a BPM requires considerable insight into all the elements of the brands, both inside the company and beyond its walls. When it's complete, a well-crafted BPM reveals potential areas of value creation and destruction, opportunities for greater returns, and risk vulnerabilities. Users can view the portfolio in three dimensions. They can spin it, approximating the perspectives of different consumer groups; they can change underlying assumptions to test economic and marketing hypotheses and shifts in consumer behavior or the basis for competition; and they can change data to test the effects of new strategies, a different brand lineup, new partnerships, and so forth.

Most large companies own hundreds of brands and have at least as many strategic partnerships. Even small companies with a limited product line like Iams, the pet food company, own more than a hundred brands.[1] We don't need to create huge polymer-like molecules composed of hundreds and hundreds of brands. We need map only the set of brands that we must manage collectively. This set usually includes thirty to a hundred brands that represent a complete value proposition to a segment of customers.

The Cadillac BPM illustrates five key dimensions shared by all brand portfolio molecules:

- First, it defines all the brands that the company should consider in making brand decisions. In this molecule, we see not only the Cadillac brands, but also linked brands that affect Cadillac's strategy.

- Second, the relative value of the different brands in the portfolio in terms of each brand's contribution to influencing the target market's purchase decision is easy to see. The size of the sphere denotes value. The larger the sphere, the more important it is to the target customer. For example, in the luxury car category, the nameplate usually influences the consumer most. At the watercooler, the proud new owner says, "I just bought a Cadillac." Thus the Cadillac sphere is the largest in the portfolio and "Cadillac" is what we have termed a "lead brand."

Lead brands drive the purchase decision and loyalty. "Strategic brands" like Catera speak to specific target segments, technology, or usage occasions. "Support brands" like OnStar provide proof of the overall value proposition. On the molecule, strategic and support brands are smaller spheres than lead brands.

- Third, the brands are labeled by color (black, gray, and white) to denote their influence on the purchase decision. Not every brand helps the purchase decision, especially not in mature brand portfolios. Brands that contribute positively appear in black. Neutral brands appear gray, and negative brands appear white.[2] For example, DeVille is black even though many older consumers love this car. Younger consumers, however, who are the primary target for the brand portfolio, prefer the STS or the Escalade, which are shown in white. (In color versions green, blue, and red work particularly well.)

- Fourth, the molecule highlights how the brands in the portfolio connect—and relate—to one another. General Motors (GM) for example, owns OnStar, which is now available on Saabs and Toyotas. A Cadillac brand portfolio manager would probably not want to share a valuable differentiating feature like OnStar with other car companies, but he has little say in the matter. So the connection of OnStar to the GM sphere is thick, but the connection to Cadillac is thin.

Also outside the collective control of the brand management group are the Senior PGA Tour, with which Cadillac has long been associated; the dealers, all of whom have their own brands and ad budgets; and brands like Allante and Cimarron that don't even exist anymore, except on used car lots, in dusty parts inventory bins, and most important, in the memories of prospective customers.

- Finally, different brands have different market positionings, and so each brand's place in the molecule reflects its market position. For example, GM has always positioned DeVille very close to the core Cadillac value proposition and loyal market. Catera is positioned much farther away, with a different value proposition and aimed at a different market.

Each molecule is unique, its size and structure the result of the industry context and the accumulated brand strategies of the company. Therefore each company must handcraft its own set of BPMs using its market research libraries and accumulated organizational insights.

The BPM eliminates much of the guesswork of brand portfolio management. Because it is quantitatively based, the brand portfolio map can take the emotion out of many brand decisions. Because it can be updated, a manager can use it to model various what-if brand portfolio scenarios. The BPM is a uniquely valuable methodology, and the more complex and dynamic the portfolio, the more valuable the BPM.

The Toolkit

The BPM allows a manager to work on the entire portfolio at once, not just on individual brands: "How would the portfolio value change if I introduced a new car positioned in between Catera and Cadillac? Should I focus advertising on the Cadillac brand or on Night Vision? How can I leverage the dealer brands?" Just as a financial portfolio manager uses puts, swaps, and straddles to manage risk and liquidity, so can a brand portfolio manager manipulate her brands to enhance overall portfolio performance.

A brand portfolio manager needs three types of tools. Every portfolio should have:

- A vision for the value it intends to create and a clear set of performance objectives

- Strategic guidelines for the overall portfolio

- A set of specific working tools, tactical approaches to improve performance of the portfolio

A financial portfolio expresses its objectives in terms of risk, return, liquidity, and mix of financial products. A brand portfolio expresses its objectives in terms of risk, return, brand equity creation, strategic flexibility, and growth. But we shouldn't press this analogy too far. If the financial portfolio manager doesn't like a stock, he can just sell it. It's far harder to sell a poorly performing brand. In financial portfolios, the interactions among the individual stocks are primarily statistical ones. In brand portfolios, all sorts of interactions occur. The financial portfolio manager can map his entire portfolio on two axes, but we need the more complex brand portfolio molecule to capture the information we must have. So it's not a perfect metaphor. But it is close enough to emphasize that a brand portfolio must have its own overarching set of objectives, not simply an accumulation of the goals of the individual brands in the portfolio.

Once the brand portfolio manager sets the objectives, she can then create a set of guidelines, similar to the investment philosophy of a fund manager, that determine the strategic direction of the portfolio. Most brand families have some sort of basic guidelines covering identity. But strategic guidelines must cover much more.

In the early 1980s, the Walt Disney Company had few brand portfolio controls. Company licensing strategy emphasized full, undiscriminating exploitation of the Disney trademarks. As a result, the company had literally hundreds of deals with companies that produced everything from diapers and cars to laundry detergent and floor wax. Often, Disney gave these marketing partners wide latitude in using Disney brands.

Late in the decade, Disney instituted a major research study to assess what consumers thought of this broad usage. The response was decidedly negative. Customers who felt personal bonds with the Disney characters expressed disappointment that their widespread commercial use cheapened the beloved icons. Others resented Disney. They perceived that the fusillade of licensed goods turned children into consumers at far too early an age. In short, consumers thought Disney was exploiting not just its brands but its relationships with its customers. They thought less of both the company and the brands as a result.

In response, Disney tightened its policies on licensing and began turning away deals that did not fit its new criteria.[3] Now, every Halloween, Disney World executives willingly surrender share to nearby Universal Studios. They do so because their guidelines clearly spell out that the Disney brand is "about children and people who are children at heart." They say, explicitly,

"We always have to be aware of our image."[4] Disney interprets this to mean that gory and violent themes don't fit. In other words the psychotic clown that scares teens over at Universal belongs there, not at Disney. Along the same lines, when Disney invested in Toysmart.com, it refused to sell "toys of a destructive nature" and instead devoted $21 million in advertising what it termed "good toys."[5]

All brand portfolios have identity manuals; few have clear, coherent guidelines to cover such things as alliances and product range. Consequently, too many are overadministered and undermanaged. A good set of brand portfolio guidelines should tackle not only details like optimal type size for magazine ads, but also tough issues like co-branding rules, allowable brand stretch, size of the portfolio, and so forth. The guidelines should be clear and uncompromising.

Of course, even vision and strategic guidelines are not enough. Every brand portfolio manager must also know how to use the eight types of portfolio tactics: extensions, repositioning, pruning, over-branding, co-branding, amalgamation, partitioning, and scaling. Some of these tools will seem familiar because they are similar to those used by individual brand managers. But a word of caution: using a hammer in outer space is not the same as using that same hammer on the ground. Using familiar tools in unfamiliar ways requires new learning—and practice. We'll look at each tool in turn and discuss when and how to use it in Part 2.

The New Organization

Finally, adopting a brand portfolio approach calls for a new type of organization. First, such a move necessitates the creation of a new role in the organization, the brand portfolio manager, whose activities extend far beyond mediating disputes between business units on how to use the logo. The brand portfolio manger must be a strategic activist who proactively shapes the size and structure of the brand portfolio.

Second, the new model elevates and changes the role of the brand manager. Today, brand managers often find themselves in conflict with overall portfolio strategy. Consider Pontiac. Pontiac's brand positioning is "Driving Excitement," and each car line brand in the portfolio must reflect the "excitement" theme. How individual managers choose to conform, however, varies widely. For example, in 1998, Pontiac spent more than $100 million to introduce the new Grand Am under the tag "Excitement Well Built." Those words more or less supported the theme, but most of the advertising copy focused heavily on the "solid" construction of the car to offset target customer perceptions that Pontiac's craftsmanship was inferior to rivals Toyota and Honda. The problem? This emphasis immediately conveyed a less "excitement-oriented" message.[6]

Bonneville, another car in the Pontiac line, comes closer to supporting the overall idea behind excitement but its advertising is also not quite in sync. Bonneville uses the tagline: "Luxury with attitude." The company's Web site touts the model as "an alternative to traditional luxury cars." The brand advertising and the brand portfolio strategy are not pulling together.

We don't mean to pick on Bonneville or Pontiac, or GM for that matter. Most organizations develop strategy piecemeal at the brand level, and then assemble the pieces like a jigsaw puzzle—and an overall picture does not always emerge. To its credit, Pontiac's brand team tried to address the portfolio issues head on. It failed because it should have approached the problem 180 degrees from where it started. In brand portfolio management, individual brand managers significantly influence the overall portfolio strategy at the outset. Then their efforts in delivering their plan work powerfully at the portfolio level first, and the individual level second.

Brand portfolio management also takes branding beyond the walls of the marketing department. Earlier, we cited the expanding definition of brand. Once the definition of brand exceeds the product and includes (or subsumes) the whole buying experience and multiple brands, everyone in the organization really has to understand what the brand represents and how to deliver it because everyone is responsible for it.

Automaker Saturn rarely makes quality superiority claims over other cars. Its basic quality and safety assurance is part and parcel of something broader and warmer: membership in the

Saturn Family. Saturn makes sure that Saturn owners never regret their purchase all through the lives of their cars. Owners get periodic correspondence, reminding them of their Saturn "anniversary" and offering discounts on checkups at the dealer garage or any local Saturn shop across the country. Saturn invites its owners to local "Saturn Family" barbecues. In June 1994, some 44,000 Saturn owners, not counting each owner's family members, returned the affection by attending a "Saturn Homecoming" at the Spring Hill, Tennessee, plant.

For Saturn, the brand does not stop at what the company does. It's what the company is. The brand has become the knowledge spine around which the company organizes all the other components of the business. Scott Bedbury of Starbucks says, "That's what a well-defined, well-articulated brand is to a company, to its customers, even its employees. Employees want to love the company they work for, and if they do—big surprise—they do better work. When I was at Nike, there were athletes who took one-fourth of what Reebok was offering to wear our shoes, because they believed in what we stood for. All of a sudden, the brand is about more than just marketing."[7]

Companies like Gateway, the computer maker, involve everyone in marketing execution by requiring corporate employees personally to answer customer letters, calls, and e-mails. Starbucks chief executive officer (CEO), Howard Schultz, considers his 37,000 employees "brand ambassadors," even calling them "partners" in benefit plan materials. These workers directly interface with the people who come in the door every day. They provide the pleasurable experience that is part of the pull that will bring the customers back again. Starbucks trains its employees with detailed knowledge of the company's exotic fare so that they can offer suggestions based on a customer's tastes and mood.[8] In brand-based business models using brand portfolio approaches, the whole company is the marketing department.

For the rest of this book we discuss these three elements— the portfolio approach, the toolkit, and executing the organization and culture to make it happen.

3

the molecule in detail

By convention there is color, by convention sweetness, by convention bitterness. But in reality, there are atoms and space.
—Democritus, *c. 400* BC

MAPPING A BRAND PORTFOLIO MOLECULE is tough because to do it right means tossing out most of your ingrained understanding about your brands and how they are positioned. You must make a fresh start and think about your brands only from the customer's point of view. In other words, you have to distance yourself from the way in which you and your company think of your brands, their current positioning, and their organizational boundaries between brand managers.

The first step is taking inventory. What brands should you include in your brand portfolio molecule? What brands influence the customer's decision to purchase what you have to offer?

Consider Harley-Davidson motorcycles. If you were in the market for a large, chrome-plated cruising motorcycle, you'd probably trek to a Harley dealer. Once you got there, though, you'd find that Harley also owns and sells Buell motorcycles, a line of sleek, low-slung vehicles. What's more, you would quickly learn that Harley doesn't have just a single brand of road cruisers; numerous individual brands reside under the name and even more brand extensions under those. You can't buy just a Harley. You have to choose among a Dyna, a Softail, a Sportster, a Touring, or a Fat Boy. Breaking it down further, if you select a Dyna, you have to decide whether you want a Dyna FX, FXDXT, FXDX, FXDL, FXDWG, or FXD.

The Harley brand portfolio is fairly typical of many in that it also embraces a host of ancillary brands that do not represent the actual products. HOG, for instance, is the Harley Owner's Group. The Harley-Davidson Café is a restaurant in midtown Manhattan. Harley has trademarked the term Motorclothes—another brand—to describe its line of clothing accessories, which it promotes heavily. Then there's Rider's Edge, the company's official riding school. Not to mention some six hundred dealers of the Harley cycles, each of which has its own brand that connects in some way to Harley, influencing it positively or negatively, adding some flavor of its own to the central brand.

But that's not all. Consider the new Harley Ford truck, which provides a bridge between the core Harley portfolio and the sprawling Ford brand portfolio.

And what about the offshoots? American Ironhorse makes its own line of motorcycles that start with a power train and frame supplied by Harley. Harley Mom, a trademark-protected Web site, exists so that Harley riders can find and communicate with one another. There are too many clubs, semiofficial organizations, and publications that connect in some way to the Harley brand to count. What's more, a plethora of other companies make clothes, or posters, or motorcycle parts, all of which in some way have a connection with—and an effect on—the Harley name. And if you're the person at Harley trying to inventory out the company's brand portfolio, you must acknowledge all of the above! Because every single brand we've mentioned—product, company, club, whatever—is important to Harley's core target market and thus important enough to include in the portfolio.

Simply listing the brands in any portfolio is a challenging exercise. How can it be so difficult? Well, to begin, it takes a fair bit of digging to find all the brands involved. Brand portfolios are so large and complex that no manager can rattle the whole list off the top of her head. Nor can you just grab the trademark list. Trademark lists often contain duplications and redundancies, and seldom include the names of important marketing partners. American IronHorse motorcycles, for example, wouldn't show up on a list of Harley-Davidson-owned trademarks, but they clearly are part of the broader brand portfolio. We also cannot overlook *American Rider,* a magazine about Harleys.

It can take weeks, in fact, to identify all the brands that might earn a place in the portfolio and then to decide whether each is in or out. Brands that play a role in the purchase decision for the target customer are in. Brands that don't are out. But it's not easy to make that call *a priori.* Oftentimes making the final call requires sifting through old market research or commissioning new studies. Building the inventory is an iterative and often hard-fought process.

But the work, however difficult, has real benefits. Not only does it force you to rethink the traditional boundaries of brand portfolios, but it also forces you to do so from the perspective of the customer, which is, of course, where all brand work should begin and end. Ultimately, if you're thinking the way the customers think, you'll have a clearer way to make decisions. You'll be able to substitute substance, in the form of customer data, for process and internal perception, which is what too many companies rely on to guide their marketing efforts. The "art" of marketing will inch that much closer to being a science.

Classification

You have an inventory of brands—congratulations. Now, unfortunately, the work gets harder, not easier. What role does each brand play? How does each influence the others? What degree of influence does each one have on the purchase decision of any other in the group? As we said in chapter 2, some of the brands you've amassed will be leaders, some will be strategic, and some will be supportive. We'll talk more in chapter 4 about the exact importance of those labels. At this point, the main idea is that some brands drive purchase and some help out. Some brands will have a positive effect on the group. Some will have a positive effect on certain other brands and a negative effect on one or two. Some will be neutral. You get the gist.

Now, how to do it. You can look at brand roles in a variety of ways. Using branding language that is fairly well known in the industry, brands can be umbrellas or master brands or sub-brands, stand-alone or freestanding brands, drivers or fighters, or silver bullets. All of these perspectives come in handy in some situations. But let's focus on how heavily different brand elements weigh in the purchase decision.

Research has shown that consumers never use all the available information in making a choice.[1] In one study, when confronted with eighteen pieces of information with which to make a purchase choice, consumers used four. In an experiment with toothpaste, buyers cited brand as the most widely used factor, price second, and the name of the manufacturer twelfth. Further, they selected the first criterion almost twice as often as the second through sixth criteria. And they chose the last eleven criteria only half as often as the secondary criteria. Yes, some consumers found these last criteria important, but most saw them as peripheral and many wrote them off as completely extraneous. In fact, the information variables clustered into three distinct tiers: *usually important, important to some people at some times,* and *usually unimportant to most consumers.*

Our client experience confirms that consumers also place brands in tiers. Precious few really drive the consumer choice, a number of others help confirm it, and still more matter to some consumers some of the time. But consumers seldom use all of a portfolio's brands in their decisions, and they never use all of the brands with equal weight.

In mapping the brand portfolio, you must glean which brands carry what weight. Every brand portfolio has a lead brand, and usually *just* one, serving as its nucleus. Often, as in the case of Harley-Davidson, the lead is self-evident. But occasionally it is not so obvious, as, for example, in the espn.go.com portfolio, a polyglot offering of Go.com, ESPN, ABC, ABC Sports, and, more covertly, Disney.

Customers cannot overlook or ignore a lead brand. It always plays some role in their decision, and customers will typically consider it twice as important as any other brand in the portfolio.

Strategic brands also carry a good deal of weight in the purchase decision at multiple points along the choice process. For example, these secondary brands often serve as attractors to pull potential new users into the brand portfolio, just as Catera lured thousands into showrooms who had never before thought of driving a Cadillac. Support brands for their part tend to cement the decision, adding that little bit of weight at the end of the process that tips the buyer over the edge.

The Map

The inventory and classification process can take from days to weeks to accomplish. Done well, it requires sifting through and analyzing reams of market research data. But after this exhaustive setup, you will be able to begin constructing a viable brand portfolio map. And in the process, you may not only learn a great deal about your business, but also cull information and insights vital to running it.

From the map comes the ability to set portfolio strategy in a dynamic way. You can challenge existing strategies, identify product holes, allocate marketing funds, and do almost any marketing task we can think of, all off this one analytical backbone. By managing brands together you will turn them from individuals into a team, a single group working to accomplish a single set of objectives.

When we originated the idea of brand portfolio mapping, we wrestled long and hard with how to actually create the map. At first, we envisioned a computer program that would take a set of coordinates and spit out a polished graphic. A company in the United Kingdom that makes CAD/CAM software for chemical companies said, "No problem," until they really dug in. Then they called back and said, "No thanks."

The basics of deciding what is in the molecule, the different brand roles, and the relationships among the brands are very straightforward. And that's 80 percent of the map. But the challenge comes in the last 20 percent, when you fold in the positioning of each brand relative to the others. That requires quantifying the positioning of each brand along three dimensions—not an easy task, to say the least. Below we discuss how we created the Cadillac map you saw in the chapter 2 and talk through how we dealt with the positioning challenge.

The Cadillac Portfolio

Let's first revisit the Cadillac brand portfolio.

For much of the twentieth century, Cadillac dominated the U.S. luxury car market. As recently as 1994, Cadillac sold 210,686 cars and was the clear leader, with a market share of over 30 percent. However, since then Cadillac has slipped precipitously. By 1999, Cadillac had slid to third in the rankings, behind Mercedes and Lexus, with Lincoln and BMW close behind. Cadillac's share in 1999 was down to just above 17 percent. In a market that grew 50 percent over that time span, Cadillac's volume shrank by 15 percent.[2]

As of this writing, Cadillac's overall portfolio plan is to bring new customers in via a few slicker offerings, while retaining the older, more traditional customer base with the Eldorado and the DeVille. Cadillac has a number of initiatives underway to execute this strategy. First, it has launched two major new products, the Catera and the Escalade, and is systematically revamping the rest of the line. Second, to make the image of the brand more youthful, Cadillac advertising now emphasizes the extraordinary technology embedded in the new vehicles. This marketing focuses on a series of branded features, including StabiliTrak, OnStar, Northstar, and Night Vision. Finally, to drive innovation and responsiveness, Cadillac has instituted what it terms "brand management," with separate marketing managers and budgets for each major product line (e.g., Seville, Catera, etc.).[3] But Cadillac's customer base is aging, and the brand has not yet shown an ability to renew itself by attracting a new, younger customer base, as have competitors such as Mercedes and BMW. Despite higher price points, the average age of a Mercedes or BMW driver is years less than that of a Cadillac buyer. As a result, Cadillac faces serious and persistent share erosion.

The Cadillac brand portfolio contains about a dozen familiar brands including GM, Cadillac, "Caddie," Seville, DeVille, Eldorado, Catera, Escalade, and Evoq. We say about a dozen because, as in the Harley case, just a little digging exposes numerous other brands connected in some way with the core brand portfolio. For example, each major product line breaks down into its own menu of models. For DeVille, there is the DHS and the DTS. For Seville, there is the SLS and the STS, which are very different cars. For Catera, there is the Steinmetz Catera, a more aggressive driving car engineered for Catera by Steinmetz-Opel in Germany.

The portfolio also contains well-known branded features, such as OnStar and StabiliTrak, and less well known "ingredient brands" exclusive to Cadillac, such as Magnasteer, Twilight Sentinel, Northstar, Night Vision, and the PASS-Key II security system. The list wouldn't be complete without a mention of Zebrano wood, the stuff of luxury interiors. A number of other ingredient brands in the portfolio do not belong solely to GM or Cadillac but show up in Cadillac marketing. The Bose Acoustimass sound system, Bosch brakes, and Michelin tires are examples.

Even though Cadillac is not a particularly complex portfolio, the boundaries are a bit unclear. Many other brands claim strong associations. Large dealers, such as New York's Potamkin, deploy substantial marketing communications budgets of their own. And Cadillac interlinks with other brand portfolios through its marketing efforts. The brand, for example, has become virtually synonymous with the Senior PGA Golf Tour, sponsoring the tour, individual events, and a team of golfers that includes Arnold Palmer, Lee Trevino, and Tom Watson. Cadillac also sponsors several golfers on the regular tours, as well as the Executive Women's Golf Association (EWGA). It holds the status of official car of the Pebble Beach golf resort. Such relationships can create powerful linkages in customers' minds, especially when sustained over long periods of time, as Cadillac has sustained its golf associations.

But that's not all. No matter how much money Cadillac spends on advertising its great new technology, the Ghost of Cadillac Past always lurks around the edges of the current portfolio, and must be given due consideration. Customers still remember the Fleetwood, the Cimarron, and the Allante—not so good. They remember the association of Cadillac with cultural icons like Aretha Franklin's "Freeway of Love," Bruce Springsteen's "Pink Cadillac," and legendary Caddie owners such as Elvis Presley—much better. (Icons like Elvis anchor virtual brand portfolios in their own right.)

Admittedly, it seems a bit far-fetched to consider Elvis when analyzing the Cadillac portfolio, but whether we end up mapping Brand Elvis somewhere on our molecular periphery or not, it must be acknowledged. Indeed, the major marketing challenge for Cadillac over the last thirty years has been less how to position its brand portfolio vis-à-vis Mercedes and more how to manage its heritage, which places huge constraints on the brand today and has thus far proved impossible to capitalize on.

Does inventorying such a portfolio really require us to consider all these elements? As we can see in table 3-1, the answer is absolutely yes. While some of these components may drop off the final brand map, the emphasis must be on completeness at this early stage. Remember we must include any brand that factors into the *consumer* decision-making process. All of the brands just listed would seem to fit that criterion.

And so, an initial inventory of the portfolio suggests thirty-seven elements, many not obvious in our first pass. Now that we have captured most of the elements of the portfolio (we hope; inventories typically go through at least four iterations before we achieve an acceptable level of completeness) we can begin ordering the different elements in a way that makes sense. When marketers first began thinking of brand systems, they initially looked to define brand identity hierarchies. They called them brand architecture diagrams or brand trees. At the top sat the corporate brand. Beneath lay product brands and brand extensions, all the way down to branded features or ingredients.[4]

Simple hierarchies, such as the one shown in table 3-2, are a useful way to begin to organize the data. We can see that Seville, Eldorado, Catera, Escalade, DeVille, Fleetwood, Allante, and Cimarron are all clearly line brands. DHS, STS, and Evoq are product brands, GM is a corporate or endorser brand, Stabili-Trak is an ingredient brand, and so on.

At this point, we can sneak ahead and begin thinking about the relationships among the different brands at the most basic level. In the Cadillac case, other than company organization, the most obvious relationships trace to how various brands fall within the immediate control of Cadillac brand portfolio managers, or don't. Roughly a third of the brands in the Cadillac portfolio are not entirely controlled by the Cadillac brand management group. The managers share features such as Bose with numerous competing car companies, including Acura. They share OnStar, the onboard navigation system much touted in Cadillac advertising, with other GM divisions and, soon, even with Toyota, in its U.S. models. Also, while Cadillac certainly may exercise influence over events it sponsors such as the Senior PGA Tour and other elements such as the dealer network, it does not control them.

So even at the inventory stage, we can start to gain insights about the portfolio, notably how much of it we *don't* control. Second, the Cadillac portfolio includes a large number of peripheral but *big* brands—GM, the Senior PGA Tour, Elvis, and so on. Contrast this with the Harley portfolio, with which Cadillac is often compared (in fact, Cadillac managers have studied the Harley case in search of new marketing ideas). Unlike the Cadillac portfolio, Harley's portfolio involves a huge number of smaller brands, many of which it doesn't control. Harley has few big strongly linked partners to worry about. Despite superficial similarities—for example, the companies were established within a year of each other—the Cadillac portfolio is very different from the Harley portfolio.

TABLE 3-1

Initial Brand Inventory: Cadillac

Owned	Not Owned
Caddie	Bosch
Cadillac	Bose
	Elvis Presley
	EWGA
	Le Mans Racing
	Michelin
	Pebble Beach
	PGA
	Potamkin (etc.)
	Senior PGA Tour
	Toyota
Allante	General Motors
Catera	
Cimarron	
DeVille	
Eldorado	
Escalade	
Fleetwood	
Seville	
Team Cadillac	
DHS	
DTS	
Evoq	
SLS	
STS	
Magnasteer	
Night Vision	
Northstar	
OnStar	
PASS-Key II	
StabiliTrak	
Steinmetz-Opel	
Twilight Sentinel	
Zebrano wood	

Table 3-1 is an initial inventory of brands for the Cadillac brand portfolio molecule. The table lists those brands that are owned by Cadillac, and those that are not.

TABLE 3-2

Cadillac Brand Hierarchy: Traditional View

	Owned	*Not Owned*
Endorser		General Motors
Master	Caddie Cadillac	Bosch Bose Elvis Presley EWGA Le Mans Racing Michelin Pebble Beach PGA Potamkin (etc.) Senior PGA Tour Toyota
Line	Allante Catera Cimarron DeVille Eldorado Escalade Fleetwood Seville Team Cadillac	
Product	DHS DTS Evoq SLS STS	
Ingredient	Magnasteer Night Vision Northstar OnStar PASS-Key II StabiliTrak Steinmetz-Opel Twilight Sentinel Zebrano wood	

Table 3-2 takes the initial inventory of Cadillac brands from table 3-1 and categorizes them into a traditional hierarchy. Five generic types of brand categories are used: endorser, master, line, product, and ingredient.

Now let's turn to classification. Different brands contribute at different levels and in different ways. OnStar and Night Vision are both ingredient brands in a traditional hierarchy, but in a BPM it is possible for one to be a support brand and the other a strategic or even a lead brand, depending on how important they have become to the Caddie buyer.

Once we recut the brand inventory in this way, it looks far different than it did in a simple hierarchy.

In the reprioritized brand portfolio map (shown in table 3-3), "General Motors," which stood at the top of the simple hierarchy, drops to the bottom. STS, a model with a distinct and strong positioning, becomes a strategic brand, while its sister product, SLS, becomes a support brand. Some of the "branded features" or "ingredients," such as Night Vision, actually stack up as strategic brands. So just by simply redefining how we rank brands, we get a completely different view of the brand portfolio.

A word of caution is appropriate here. For this example, we simply classified the brands based on our knowledge of the Cadillac brand portfolio gained from studying it extensively. However, to construct a robust and rigorous brand portfolio map takes quantitative data about a brand portfolio, its competitors, and how buyers make their decisions to switch between brands and models. This is not a warning "not to try this at home." The whole point of this book is to get you to try it. But keep in mind, you'll need all the data and information you can muster to get a viable, useful result.

Ironically, it is unlikely that the Cadillac brand management team would agree with our take on the Cadillac portfolio and, in particular, on the brand ranking. First, the designation of brands as lead, strategic, or support almost always becomes a point of contention. The designation of lead brand poses distinct implications for how companies allocate budgets and set authority flowcharts. For the individual manager of Catera, managing it as a lead brand versus a strategic brand makes all the difference in the world in terms of budget and autonomy.

But it helps to remember the definition of the lead: the main thing to which customers gravitate. Our research suggests that customers tend to choose luxury cars first by nameplate. That is, few people say, "I'm trying to choose between a luxury car by DaimlerChrysler and one by General Motors." Nor do they stand around at the gym and say, "Well, I'm going for the STS or the 528i." Rather, they most often first choose to buy a Cadillac or a Mercedes or a Lexus and then focus on the specific model. Even if the STS attracts them, they still must feel comfortable with the notion of driving a Cadillac. Regardless of the customer, the Cadillac brand plays a major role in the decision.

TABLE 3-3

The Cadillac Brand Hierarchy: BPM-Driven Inventory

	Degree of Brand Control		
Brand Roll	*High*	*Medium*	*Low*
Lead	Cadillac		
Strategic	Caddie	Evoq	Elvis Presley
	Catera	Potamkin (etc.)	Night Vision
	Eldorado	StabiliTrak	Northstar
	Escalade		OnStar
	Seville		
	STS		
Support	DeVille	Team Cadillac	Allante
	DHS		Bose
	DTS		Bosch
	SLS		Cimarron
			EWGA
			Fleetwood
			General Motors
			Le Mans Racing
			Magnasteer
			Michelin
			PASS-Key II
			Pebble Beach
			PGA
			Senior PGA Tour
			Steinmetz-Opel
			Toyota
			Twilight Sentinel
			Zebrano wood

Table 3-3 takes the traditional brand hierarchy that was presented in table 3-2 and recategorizes the brand set into a BPM-driven inventory. Specifically, each brand is designated a role, and is then classified in terms of the Cadillac brand manager's ability to control it. Notice the profound difference in classification between table 3-3 and table 3-1.

This is not the case in other categories, including some other automotive categories. For example, in the Corvette brand portfolio, Corvette is the lead brand and Chevrolet a support brand. No one ever says, "Well, I think I want a Chevrolet. Should I get an Impala, an S-10 pickup, or a Corvette?"

Earlier we said that brands can be attractors, which implies a positive role in the selling process. In fact, every brand in the portfolio is either positive, negative, or passive. Brands convey information, whether the brand manager wants them to or not. For almost all buyers, Cimarron has negative connotations. Thank goodness for Cadillac that we can chalk the Cimarron off as peripheral both in positioning and in customer importance, and thus relatively passive. Unfortunately, for many potential Cadillac buyers, DeVille is also a negative brand, and it is neither passive nor peripheral.

We want to make one final point on roles. Many elements in the Cadillac brand portfolio connect to other portfolios. That is, they are "nodes." GM is a node to many other portfolios, as is Potamkin. Bose is a node to Acura, although since it is peripheral, it is not a particularly important one. OnStar is a node, and a potentially dangerous one, since it connects to potential competitors such as Oldsmobile, as well as linking to brand portfolios with value propositions distinctly at odds with Cadillac's—for example, Saab and Toyota. Nodes can exist at any level.

To sum up our work thus far, let's consider the first-cut brand molecule shown in figure 3-1. While it lacks the full richness of the final map, it does manage to get all the brands on a single page. And by using various type sizes and distances, we begin to portray the relative importance of the different brands and the ways in which the brands relate to one another. This first-cut map also looks like something from chemistry class, and here's an important point. It might take months to develop a molecule that delivers the full power of this approach, but most managers can build a first-cut map in weeks. And there's a lot to be learned even at this stage.

Building on the first cut, we can develop the full molecule shown in figure 3-2. As we stated earlier, the trick is to capture the positioning. At this point, we did it by assigning sectors of the molecules to different types of brands. That is, we assigned

FIGURE 3-1

First-Cut Brand Portfolio Molecule: Cadillac, 2000

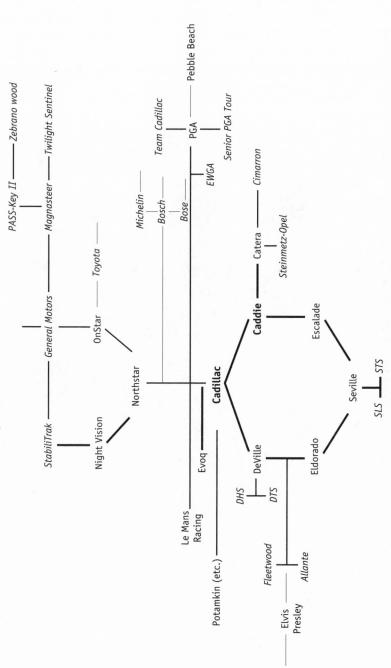

Figure 3-1 is a first-cut BPM. It was created using simple presentation software (PowerPoint), and can be hand drawn as well. It captures the same five dimensions from figure 2-1 in a simpler (albeit less visual) representation.

FIGURE 3-2

Brand Portfolio Molecule: Cadillac, 2000

Steinmetz-Opel

Catera
DHS
DTS

DeVille

Caddie
Seville
STS
Evoq
Le Mans Racing
SLS

Escalade

Team Cadillac

Pebble Beach
Senior PGA Tour

EWGA

PGA

Allante
Elvis Presley

Fleetwood
Cimarron
Potamkin (etc.)

Eldorado

Bose
Michelin
Cadillac

Bosch
Magnasteer
StabiliTrak
OnStar
Toyota
Northstar

Twilight Sentinel

Night Vision
Zebrano wood

General Motors

PASS-Key II

Figure 3-2 is a final BPM. It was created using 3-D modeling software.

"ghost brands" to a sector, competitor brands to another sector, and so on.[5] However, we want to emphasize that the process is quantifiable and analytical, not merely artistic.

The result is a means of seeing the portfolio from a whole new vantage point. Caddie, for example, bears an intense relationship to Cadillac, so intense that Caddie lies virtually on top of the Cadillac brand and shows up almost as bump on the Cadillac sphere. DeVille, in the minds of many virtually synonymous with Cadillac, lies close to the Cadillac sphere. Catera, in contrast, lies much farther away, since the division has positioned it deliberately at odds with the positioning of the main Cadillac brand. It was no accident that Cadillac advertising labeled Catera "the Caddie that zigs" and mocked the duck in the famous Cadillac emblem by turning it into a "spokescartoon." Still, Catera is undeniably a Caddie. It wears the Cadillac badge, leverages the Cadillac name in its advertising, and sells through Cadillac dealers. Some suspect it has even cannibalized the existing Cadillac line in some areas.

What else does the map tell us? Look at it as a whole. First, the relative size of the Cadillac sphere suggests that any market-ing effort, to be successful, must focus on the base Cadillac brand itself. The strategy of supporting individual brands will not restore share growth. The second major insight is that Catera, intended to be a silver bullet brand that will single-handedly pull the Cadillac brand portfolio toward younger cus-tomers, is unlikely to do the trick. It may well be a successful car if judged as its own island, but it simply lacks enough mass to move the huge Cadillac portfolio. For Catera to do its strategic job, Cadillac must place a hugely disproportionate amount of resources behind it. A more successful strategy might well be to use a silver bullet, but one a bit closer to the core positioning, as Apple did with iMac. A third implication is that any money spent to hype the features of OnStar, Northstar, et al., could prove a risky play, since the parent has shown a willingness to make those features available not only to other GM divisions (e.g., Oldsmobile and Pontiac) but also to competitors. Finally, the negative contribution of some of the older brands means that, at a minimum, Cadillac should reduce any advertising sup-port to these brands that might be seen by the "new Cadillac buyer." Probably, Cadillac should consider phasing these cars out over time. Bold conclusions all, but ones driven by data, analysis, and a more holistic view of the customer buying decisions than any previously used.

A smart brand portfolio manager, studying this map, might well reverse virtually every aspect of recent Cadillac strategy.

4

portfolio dynamics

The way a team plays as a whole determines its success. You may have the greatest bunch of individual stars in the world, but if they don't play together, the club won't be worth a dime.
—Babe Ruth

MAPPING YOUR BRAND PORTFOLIO forces you to think through brand roles, and it's a good exercise. In particular, defining roles from a consumer perspective adds a rigor to managing brands that cuts through organizational politics and injects real strategy into the discussion of what your brands are and where they're going. It also leads us to the most controversial idea in this book: brands in a portfolio need to play differentiated roles. We mentioned this idea in chapter 3, but didn't go into great detail; we're going to do that now.

Assigning different roles to your brands and aligning them to pull together means more than just setting different financial targets and marketing budgets based on growth potential. It means that optimizing the portfolio may sometimes mean suboptimizing individual brands. In financial portfolios, suboptimizing an individual stock never makes sense. In brand portfolios, sometimes it does. We'll grant you, deliberate suboptimization is not an easy idea to get your head around, but consider the following story:

For three weeks each year, 180 of the world's top cyclists race across southwest Europe in the Tour de France. Race organizers throw every type of test at the riders—long rides over flat roads, steep mountain climbs, wheel-to-wheel sprints. Each day, or stage, has a winner, but the real winner is the rider who covers the entire 2,251 miles in the lowest total time. Fifty-two different riders have won the eighty-two Tours de France. They have come in all nationalities, shapes, and sizes, but they have one thing in common. A strong team put them on the podium.

Each team is composed of a few stars and a number of lesser-known riders called *domestiques.* Domestiques surround their leader in the crowded, dangerous *peloton,* protecting him from jostles and bumps that can send him crashing down at thirty miles an hour. They ride ahead to break the wind on the plains. Often, they sacrifice their own ambitions and aspirations, expending precious energy chasing breakaway groups in the mountains, knowing that their legs will be rubber the next morning and they will labor at the back of the field.

Brand portfolio management also is a team sport. The individual brands in the portfolio exist to put the portfolio across the finish line first. Usually, if the lead brand wins, so will the entire portfolio. It does no good to win victories for individual supporting brands if as a result the portfolio gets left behind, as it did with Miller Beer.

Miller Beer is the second largest beer company in the United States. In the 1970s, the company launched an attack on market leader Anheuseur-Busch by concentrating resources behind a strategic brand, Miller Lite. Miller Lite was an almost instant hit and one of the most successful brand launches in history. Anheuseur-Busch, by contrast, focused its effort on its lead brand, Budweiser, investing less in smaller or supporting brands like its strategic entry, Bud Dry. Today, the Budweiser brand portfolio has widened its lead on the Miller brand portfolio, as shown in figure 4-1. Bud Light has even opened up a huge lead over Miller Lite,

FIGURE 4-1

Beer Production in Millions of Thirty-One Gallon Barrels
Beer Production: Budweiser vs. Miller High Life

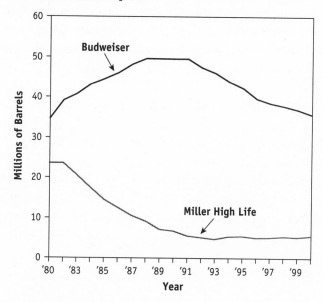

Source: *Brewer's Almanac,* The Beer Institute.

despite Miller Lite's head start and heavy media spend. Team performance has made the difference.

The Role of the Lead

Why is the lead brand so important? The lead brand defines the positioning of the portfolio. The lead carries most of the burden for making the sale or not making the sale. The lead brand centers the brand portfolio.

Usually the lead brand is obvious. Simply visualize a retail store that sells all of your brands in any one product or service category.[1] There's a sign in front of the store, with all of your brand names on it, luring consumers in. Now let's say it is necessary to paint out every single name on that sign except one. Which one would you keep?

It's true that sometimes portfolios have two or even three strong brands, making it hard to spot the lead. Callaway makes high-end golf clubs under the brands Big Bertha, Great Big Bertha, Hawk Eye, Odyssey, and so on. The Hawk Eye driver carries the strategic brand of Hawk Eye, but it also carries both the Callaway and Big Bertha brands. Both are well known and highly regarded. But which is the lead? We don't know; we would have to see the research. But chances are that Callaway doesn't know either—if it did, it probably wouldn't clutter up its golf clubs with logo upon logo like a NASCAR sedan. It would be worth it to the company to decide.

Strong leads make strong portfolios. The Jeep portfolio has a strong lead brand, and although the strategic brands do most of the heavy lifting, there is no mistaking where the company places its emphasis. In 1999, Jeep sold 680,700 units and grew at 20 percent.[2] The Dodge brand portfolio has strong strategic brands, such as the Viper, but those brands don't do what they should for the lead brand, and the portfolio falls short of its promise. In 1999, Dodge sold 1.8 million units but grew at only 4 percent.

Strategic Brands

Designating a single brand as the lead does not imply the other brands aren't important. It also doesn't imply that they should not flourish. Take strategic brands, the second "biggest" spheres in the brand molecule. Strategic brands boost the return/risk ratio in four distinct ways:

- First, they lure new users to the portfolio, as Catera did with some success for Cadillac.

- Second, they play a defensive role, blocking or responding to competitors. In the early 1990s, the Arm & Hammer brand portfolio extended into such categories as laundry detergent, cat litter, and toothpaste categories, even gaining the number three spot in toothpaste. But the number one and two brand portfolios responded quickly enough with strategic entries of their own—baking soda formulas of Crest and Colgate—to regain much of the lost ground.

- Third, strategic brands provide useful platforms on which to experiment, allowing the portfolio manager to take chances and lowering the risk of brand contamination. Over the last two decades Reebok has moved away from a focus on major sports. But in the early 1980s, it relaunched the Blacktop line of outdoor-specific basketball shoes. Similarly, the iPaq allows Compaq to test wireless products without stretching the equity of the Compaq line of desktops.

- Finally, strategic brands can effectively be used to make some noise, to attract attention to the brand portfolio without confusing the message of the lead brand. Automakers produce "halo" cars, niche models with striking styling, designed as much for the buzz as for the bottom line.3 The Mustang of 1964, VW's New Beetle, and the Mazda Miata are all halo cars. Chrysler makes the Dodge Viper, the Prowler, and now the Chrysler PT Cruiser, a retro-styled minivan with souped-up road performance. The New Beetle helped double VW sales in 1998, not only by selling heavily itself, but also by pulling in curious buyers to showrooms, where they then bought less flashy Passats and Jettas.

A great strategic brand can work toward several objectives. The most adroit use of a strategic brand in the last ten years is Apple's iMac. Everyone knows the story: Apple was at one time the leading personal computer (PC) maker in the world. However, by 1997, Apple's revenues had fallen from $11.1 billion in 1995 to $7.1 billion. In a single quarter in 1996, it managed to lose $740 million. The Newton, Apple's entry into the hand-held organizer market, hit the market ten years too early and operated clumsily. Apple lost its commanding lead in ease of use and graphics to Microsoft Windows. Indeed, the software gap between Microsoft and Apple had grown enormous.

A focus on the business sector and volume for volume's sake led to Apple computers that looked similar to the dull, uniform, putty-colored PCs that anchored row upon row of corporate workstations. The price of the stock plummeted from a high of over $36 in 1991 to just above $6. Even Mac fanatics questioned the viability of the company, which went through three CEOs and laid off 30 percent of its staff.[4]

As we write, Apple's stock price has rebounded. The company's biggest problem is meeting demand for its aesthetically breathtaking new line of products.[5] Competitors, once again, copy Macintosh designs and marketing. A single extraordinary strategic brand, the iMac, has driven much of the success. Launched in August 1998, the iMac didn't look like other computers and it didn't perform like other computers. Instead of standard, boring beige, the iMac came in "Bondi Blue." Five months later came five new colors: Blueberry, Strawberry, Lime, Tangerine, and Grape. In summer 2000 came Graphite, Indigo, Ruby, Snow, and Sage. But the big thing about iMac was that it was designed specifically to be user-friendly—like the original Mac—and, more important at the time, anyone with an iMac could hook it up quickly and log on to the Internet in about four minutes by following an ultrasimple set of instructions. (Aficionados claimed that part of those four minutes was spent looking for scissors to cut the tape on the box.[6]) As Jeff Goldblum crowed in a voiceover on one of the iMac's televised launch spots: "There's no 'Step 3!'"

From its launch, the iMac led all PC models in retail shipments every month through the end of 1998. By 1999, Apple's share of desktop computer retail sales had hit 4.7 percent, twice that of a year earlier, according to ZD Market Intelligence (ZDMI). The buzz around the iMac lifted the entire brand portfolio, with ZDMI estimating, at one point in the launch period, that under the halo of its launch, sales of other Apple products rose a remarkable 20 percent. Even more telling, in early 1999, industry estimates had new PC buyers and Wintel (IBM-compatible, Microsoft-software-based PCs) converts together accounting for 50 percent or more of iMac purchases. In 1999, Apple sales growth continued apace, jumping 25 percent in unit sales and 3 percent in net sales, to $6.1 billion.[7] *MC* magazine, in naming Apple its Marketer of the Year in 1999, declared iMac a sort of zen messiah for the company: "The iMac is a hit for making Apple Apple again."[8]

The iMac is a textbook case on using strategic brands. It attracted both attention and new users to the portfolio. It allowed Apple to experiment with new designs and blocked competitors from using Internet-access tools to woo away loyal Apple users. The iMac as strategic brand worked in part because it was unmistakably different from any other computer in the world. It looked different, even from other Macs, in its colors and its half-egg shape, and because the computer and monitor came in the same console, it eliminated a lot of cable stringing.

But the brand also served as an exemplary strategic entry because it successfully walked the fine line between being different and, at the same time, clearly and staunchly representing the promise of the brand portfolio.

It's a hard act. If the positioning is too close, a strategic brand can simply cannibalize the existing portfolio. And if it is too distant, the danger is that it won't embody the brand. As Thomas R. Marinelli, vice president in charge of the Jeep and Chrysler brands, puts it, launch a strategic brand that's too far removed from the core and consumers will think, "That's not really a Chrysler."[9]

Support Brands

Support brands serve as brand portfolio cement, sealing the deal, removing objections to the sale, tipping potential buyers over the edge. They're the brands that highlight a specific feature, ingredient, or benefit and, as a result, more finely segment the market, substantially increasing the likelihood that someone will buy from your line. Tylenol, for example, has branded formulations for sinus headaches, colds, flu, sore throat, allergies, arthritis, and sleeping difficulties. Multiple support brands attract the consumer in the cold-and-flu aisle by citing specific symptoms and increase the chances the consumer will remember the line at some point in the future when different symptoms manifest.

A support brand can put a resounding oomph in a brand portfolio when and where it's most needed. Frito-Lay uses the Wow support brand to augment traditional Frito-Lay brands such as Ruffles, Lay's, and Doritos.

Support brands must be used sparingly. As we will see in chapter 15, Cadillac now sits awash in component, technology, and ingredient brands, one of which, its OnStar navigation system, has even been given its own dedicated, big-budget ad campaign, independent of Cadillac. Misuse occasionally even creates high comedy. When actor Ricardo Montalban solemnly told consumers to buy the Chrysler Cordoba because of its "fine Corinthian leather," the line was parodied by comedians and the public for years thereafter.

Synchronicity

As we've said, brand portfolios as we see them contain not just brands sold by one manufacturer, but also any other brands that affect the way a consumer perceives your brand. In that spirit, you can use support brands that belong to someone else to strengthen the portfolio. Scores of manufacturers have tapped the DuPont brand portfolio for support brands: for example, Lycra and Dacron (apparel), Teflon and SilverStone (cookware), Stainmaster (carpets), and Surlyn (golf balls). (You should use other people's brands carefully though, because doing so can result in a transfer of brand equity from your portfolio to theirs. This has happened in PCs, where Intel has now become a bigger brand than many of the lead brands of the PCs that use its chips. We will discuss this issue in more depth in chapter 11, which covers co-branding.)

The real power of brand portfolios lies in how different brands work together. The Apple lead brand provides the consumer base into which to launch iMac; "iMac" itself delivers on the strategic brand agenda. Apple surrounded iMac with support brands that removed possible objections to the sale. Steve Jobs made a brilliant move when he struck a deal with Microsoft, opening the Apple system up to traditional Wintel PC software developers after years of being locked out format-wise from some of the best software on the market. What's more, hot-selling games, such as Id's Quake III, are being released for the first time in Windows and Mac versions simultaneously. Now, such brands—even Microsoft Word—support the portfolio while linking it positively to other portfolios. The iMac purchaser could not get online as quickly if AOL, through a node deal, was not ready and waiting on the iMac as soon as he turned it on.[10]

Now new strategic brands like the G4 have joined the iMac in the Macintosh portfolio. The G4 Cube and the svelte, many-colored iBook laptop offerings, like the original, look like *nothing* in their product category. Even now, the company is advertising a sleek, new, iMac-design-friendly Optical Mouse, a machine that tracks your hand movements without a little ball inside clogging up over time.

Sorting brands into lead, strategic, and support is a crucial step in optimizing the portfolio. It is also a step that requires constant revisiting. In Part 3, we will talk more about setting objectives that tie brand efforts together and about organizing to deliver these objectives. Before doing that, however, we want to stay at the brand portfolio level a little longer and discuss how to shape the size and structure of the portfolio.

5

how brand
portfolios differ

*I speak without exaggeration when I say that I have
constructed three thousand different theories in connection with
the electric light, yet only in two cases did my experiments prove
the truth of my theory.*
—Thomas Alva Edison, *1878*

B y NOW, you may have ignored our advice against
quick-and-dirty brand portfolio mapping and sketched
your own molecule up on a whiteboard. (Great!) If you
have—or even if you're just noodling around with the
idea in your mind, you'll quickly notice that your portfolio molecule doesn't look exactly like the Cadillac example shown in chapters 2 and 3.

Don't worry, it shouldn't. Brand portfolios are like
snowflakes. No two look exactly alike, behave exactly
alike, or are exactly alike. Each brand portfolio starts from
a different place in terms of product range and customers.
Each is shaped and reshaped by the forces of communication, competitive pressure, customer base evolution,
trade partner interactions, product and technology

evolution, and, perhaps most important, strategic and managerial decisions. The final result is something completely unique to your company. Both its size and structure are different from anyone else's. The starting point is always a line of products and services, usually offered in one category and created and grown inside company halls. But as they grow, external forces also play a part, morphing their size and structure. Ultimately, both sets of factors affect the final portfolio and show up in size, structure, and inter-connectedness.

External Forces

External factors affect your brand portfolio in a very dynamic way. Competitors launch products, for example, and your portfolio must respond. In 1993, P&G was blindsided by Chesebrough-Pond's (Unilever's) Mentadent, a foaming, baking soda-and-peroxide toothpaste, and eventually was forced to respond with a number of new value-added dentifrices or lose loyal Crest users to a competing brand portfolio.

New technologies also spur the creation of new brands, extensions, and alliances. For example, Coca-Cola already had a diet cola in 1983, Tab, but it was saccharin based. The new ingredient Nutrasweet offered a taste much closer to sugar and led to Diet Coke.

On a much broader scale, consider the effect of a merger or an acquisition—a critical external factor in today's markets. Mergers and acquisitions (M&As) slam portfolios together, changing size and structure virtually overnight. Over the last twenty years, M&A activity has been relentless.

Take a typical company in the telecommunications industry. Verizon Wireless is the largest provider of cellular services in the United States, with a market share of over 28 percent. Much of this growth has come from acquisitions and mergers. In 1995, what is now Verizon was seven different wireless companies. In 1996, Bell Atlantic and NYNEX combined and two years later became simply Bell Atlantic. In 1996, Cellular Communications and Air Touch combined under the AirTouch name, which then combined with US West's cellular assets in late 1997 and then with CommNet in 1998. In 1999, this group combined with Bell Atlantic to form PrimeCo. Meanwhile, GTE was absorbing Ameritech' s Midwestern business. In 2000, GTE and Bell Atlantic combined to form Verizon. Thus, in only five years, two major new brands were launched, two portfolios were separated, and seven different brand portfolios were combined.[1]

Most companies sooner or later face some level of M&A–driven portfolio restructuring. Since 1981, the number of mergers, acquisitions, and divestitures in the United States is up almost tenfold, as shown in table 5-1.

And whenever brand portfolios are combined, each portfolio is inevitably affected, even if the intent is to keep the brands distanced from one another. Consider what happened when Zebra Technologies of Vernon Hills, Illinois, bought Eltron, a

TABLE 5-1

Complete Mergers, Acquisitions, and Divestitures

Year	Transactions
1981	943
1982	1726
1983	2860
1984	3538
1985	2154
1986	2875
1987	2995
1988	3543
1989	4607
1990	5214
1991	4498
1992	4697
1993	5128
1994	6296
1995	7561
1996	8473
1997	9027
1998	9933
1999	8109

Table 5-1 lists the total number of mergers, acquisitions, and divestitures that took place in the United States during the corresponding year. Any transactions that were unannounced or pending approval at the close of that year are not included in the annual totals.

Source: 2000 Securities Industry Factbook, Securities Industry Association.

competitor based in California, in 1998. Both companies make bar code printers. Both are extremely successful and have made numerous lists of the fastest-growing and best-managed small companies in America. Zebra's strength is in what are called bench-top printers—larger, more costly machines often used in industrial environments. Eltron is best known for its desktop models and portables. When the United Parcel Service (UPS) pickup driver prints out a bar code and sticks it on a package, chances are it is an Eltron printer supplying the label.

When they merged, the two companies made a conscious decision to adopt a "two-brand strategy." By late 2000, however, it was obvious that the strategy was not working as intended and management made the decision to pull the plug on the Eltron printer brand. (It remains in use for another line of products.)

What happened to Zebra is a classic story of what Zebra's former executive vice president of strategy, Jack LeVan, calls "the schism between strategic elegance and implementation pragmatism." The original idea was to keep the brands separate, but organizational momentum quickly forced them together. Eltron resellers wanted to carry the prestigious Zebra brand. Zebra resellers wanted a lower-priced product with the Zebra cachet. Managers looking for cost savings combined the customer service teams and consolidated advertising in the same agency. Eltron sales reps quickly added Zebra to their business cards. In no time at all, the strategy went from a "two-brand" portfolio strategy to one-and-a-half, then one.

Zebra and Eltron had no experience in keeping brands separate and managing multiple distinct brand portfolios. But don't ever underestimate the likelihood of crossover effects from a merger, even if you are the best marketer the world has ever known. Back in 1931, P&G created brand management, which calls for strict separation of brand portfolios at the marketing level. But in 1999, soon after acquiring Iams, the Dayton-based pet food company, P&G began distributing the product through grocery channels. The company also replaced Iams's ad agency with one that handles other P&G products, and installed a P&G marketer to lead Iams marketing.[2] Although these are very subtle changes, they will affect the Iams brand portfolio over time. M&As always do.

Internal Factors

One of the biggest influences on a brand portfolio is the management approach behind it. Companies in the same industry with the same customers and the same basic strategies can still have very different brand portfolios. Tricon maintains three brand molecules: Kentucky Fried Chicken (KFC), Pizza Hut, and Taco Bell. Each has a rapidly shifting calendar of promotional items and has its own distinctive menu focus and also iconography: Colonel Sanders, the distinctive red roof, and the talking Chihuahua. And yet it also bundles its brands in some retail locations, occasionally combines all three for cross-restaurant movie tie-in promotions, such as *Star Wars: Episode I*, and maintains prominent promotional relationships with its soft-drink vendor and former parent company, Pepsi.

McDonald's, by contrast, offers a broader range of foods inside one brand portfolio—hamburgers, chicken, and fish. The portfolio is very active with temporary alliances, even with its serial promotion partner, Disney, but as far as permanent tie-ups go, is far more independent.

These differences are due to both the history that shaped the parent companies and more subtle management philosophies at play. In general, companies with greater sophistication in brands tend to have explicit processes for creating and combining brands, which results in portfolios with fewer core brands. Coca-Cola, 114 years old, has only 28 owned elements in its portfolio. In 25 years, Microsoft has reached 346.

In general, most companies these days tend toward very high levels of activity at both levels—creating brands and connecting them to other portfolios. Budweiser is almost synonymous with the National Football League (NFL) through signage, long-term sponsorships, and promotions such as the Bud Bowl. The higher the levels of strategic activity, the larger and looser the portfolio will be. The higher the level of tactical activities, the more interconnected the portfolio will be to other portfolios.

The Dimensions of Diversity

Portfolios exhibit many dimensions of diversity. They differ in size—the number of different brands in the molecule; in structure—how closely they are positioned and how tightly connected; and in interconnectedness—how closely they are connected to other brand molecules.

Size. When we speak of the size of a brand portfolio, we are referring primarily to how many elements are in it. To keep it simple, just for this part of the discussion, start by considering the number of brands the company owns (what we generally call a brand system). Microsoft tallies up with 346 elements, and the GM count tops near five hundred.[3] Both would be far larger if we counted all the brands that they are allied with. The count for a typical brand portfolio—not including brands outside company ownership—falls somewhere between thirty and five hundred.

Larger portfolios are harder to manage and more costly to maintain. They offer more vulnerable flanks to competitive attack. They offer risks in terms of cross-contamination. But they also offer more opportunities for scale and growth. Nestlé becomes harder to manage when it uses the Nestlé name on every product from milk flavoring to candy bars. And yet the Nestlé name improves the likelihood of purchase across the portfolio. Size matters.

Structure. Does the brand portfolio molecule spin around a strong strategic brand, like Harley, or a weak one, like Chevrolet? Is it a relatively tight portfolio, like Iams's, with a specific technology base, value proposition, and target market for all elements of the portfolio, or is it more diffuse, like Virgin's? Is it reasonably self-contained and self-reliant, like BMW's, or is it plugged into dozens or even hundreds of other brand portfolio molecules, like Disney's? These structural dimensions determine how a brand portfolio molecule operates in the short term and contribute to whether it thrives or withers in the long term.

Highly structured molecules—tight, self-contained molecules—generally anchor to strong lead brands. Loosely structured molecules most often spin around weak lead brands, weak at least relative to the strategic brands in the portfolio, and show a relatively high ratio of nodes. Neither structure is good or bad per se, but each comes with pros and cons.

Highly structured molecules are often relatively static and depend on underlying category expansion for growth. However, they are easy to manage. Loosely structured molecules offer more opportunities, but are also more of a challenge to position, and to reposition. Repositioning such a portfolio in fact is bit like trying to fan away cigar smoke; the brands in the molecule swirl around but often don't move in the desired direction. Loosely structured molecules do tend to throw up a tremendous number of growth opportunities. But because they elude simple, easy management, these growth opportunities are often hard to realize.

While size can change in the short term—for example, if a company launches a new line or acquires a similarly focused company—structure usually takes longer to develop. It might accumulate as a function of decisions that management made, or didn't, over its entire history.

Interconnection. Interconnection of brand portfolios can be permanent or temporary. Most permanent connections are historical, as is the link between Ford and Mercury. However, increasingly, companies create connections to mine the value between portfolios. Atlanta-based The Home Depot has long been the fastest-growing hardware store in the United States. The Home Depot is what is known as a big box retailer because of its huge selection and low prices. Big boxes are a notoriously competitive retail category, and often new store chains emerge, grow large on the basis of volume purchasing and aggressive pricing, and then flounder.

The Home Depot has sustained success in a brutal category not with an emphasis just on price, but also on a carefully designed and nurtured brand portfolio strategy. The Home Depot brand, with its now familiar orange-and-white logo and distinctive store design, is well known in its own right, but what really sets it apart is its management's keen understanding of all the brands that touch on its own brand portfolio molecule.

Consider, for example, the hybrid brand the company has created in conjunction with the Scott's lawn care company and John Deere. The Home Depot exclusively sells a line of lawn mowers under the "Scott's by John Deere" name. The Scott's name is a strong asset for a lawn mower because of its strong brand in lawn fertilizer. John Deere is strong because of its long connection to heavy, reliable equipment, epitomized by its slogan "Nothing runs like a Deere." The Home Depot saw the potential for combining these two brands and played matchmaker, in the process gaining a strong brand that appears only in The Home Depot outlets.

Some companies are comfortable with this sort of brand "borrowing," others are not. The Home Depot has in essence borrowed the brand equity of these two brands to create a new one. Nor is this the first such brand The Home Depot has used to create a new line. Ridgid, a maker of tools for plumbers, has a similar arrangement whereby The Home Depot markets Ridgid Power Tools, a segment in which Ridgid never before participated. Another retailer, Kmart, leveraged the Martha Stewart brand.

Brand portfolio molecules vary greatly in the nature and number of interconnections with other portfolios. Some qualify merely as one-off promotions, as when Burger King strikes a tie-in agreement with a hit movie, say, Nickelodeon's *Rugrats*, to put toys based on the movie characters in its Kids Meal boxes. Others last much longer, as the Scott's/John Deere example above, or the longtime, subtle, but pervasive links between Nike and the National Basketball Association (NBA). Such associations don't necessarily require monogamy. Cadillac enjoys a close link to Bose, the producer of audio systems. Bose, however, also supplies and markets jointly with other car companies. The NBA maintains nearly familial links both with NBC and with Time Warner's Turner cable networks, while Nike maintains multimillion-dollar contracts with many college basketball programs and makes heavy annual media buys surrounding the NCAA basketball tournament broadcasts.

In the aggregate, the number of links a brand portfolio molecule maintains with other portfolios, and the strength of those links in terms of duration, investment, and exclusivity, forms a variable called interconnection. The higher the interconnection of the portfolio with other portfolios, the more varied the growth opportunities, the lower the level of brand portfolio molecule control, and the more difficult it is to manage.

Moving On

Callaway and PING make and market golf clubs, with great success. Both rely heavily on "killer app" technology, a constant stream of new products designed to help weekend Tiger Woodses overcome increasingly more difficult courses. Both are positioned at the higher end of the price range. Both are small companies. But notwithstanding their similarities, they operate wholly different types of brand portfolios.

The most obvious differences lie in the size and structure of their portfolios. PING's portfolio features relatively few lead and strategic brands: PING, ZING, i3, Karsten, ISI, and TiSI. Further, it features lots of support brands, all wrapped tightly around the core. "PING," obviously, holds primary status, emblazoned in huge letters on every club, and dominates the portfolio.

In contrast, Callaway markets a huge number of brands and uses them in many different ways. Callaway is the lead brand, but the case is by no means as clear-cut as PING's. Callaway's Big Bertha, Odyssey, and Hawk Eye brands, ostensibly strategic brands, all exert a mighty pull on consumer purchase decisions. Both "Callaway" and "Big Bertha," for example, appear on Hawk Eye and Steelhead clubs. Numerous peripheral brands such as White Hot, the material used as an insert on the face of one new putter, and brand variants, such as Big Bertha, Little Bertha, and Great Big Bertha, all serve to spread the brand portfolio out. Indeed, a Callaway club carries brand names large and small, across, front and side, and up and down. The company's trademark large clubs serve dual purposes, giving the golfer an equipment advantage and making it easier to document the breadth of the brand portfolio on the product itself.

Same business, different management styles, radically different brand portfolios—one is tight and small, the other large and sprawling. One has very high levels of connectedness. The other is very introverted. In chapter 6 we will look at the tools with which one optimizes a brand portfolio. We will quickly find that the tools that are most applicable to one are not necessarily best suited to another.

optimizing the

brand
portfolio

6

measuring success

When you can measure what you are speaking about, and express it in numbers, you know something about it. But when you cannot measure it, when you cannot express it in numbers, the knowledge is of a meager and unsatisfactory kind.
—Lord Kelvin, *1889*

NOW IT'S TIME to create value. Let's start by talking about it in terms of returns and risks.

Improving Returns

Before David Aaker, only trademark lawyers thought about brands. Every one agreed brands were a good thing, but no one thought much about measuring the value of the brand as a stand-alone asset.[1] Aaker insisted there was such a thing as brand equity, and to prove it, he laid out six ways that brands create value for the firms that own them. He said brands with high equity have greater efficiency and effectiveness of their marketing programs, high levels of brand loyalty, premium prices, more successful new products, greater leverage with the trade, and, overall, greater competitive advantage.[2] Aaker's thinking on brand equity fundamentally changed the way everyone thinks about branding.

Since value, in mathematical terms, is simply the discounted sum of expected future returns, we can use Aaker's basic framework to think about return to the brand portfolio as well. It's not a perfect fit, because some of the value in brands, and some of the returns to brand portfolios, are hard to quantify.[3] But it's a start.

We can assign numbers to the first four sources of returns without much difficulty. Managers can track brand loyalty and new product success by looking at volumes. Price premiums (and, more realistically in this day and age, lower levels of discounts) show up in margin. Marketing program efficiency and effectiveness lead to lower levels of marketing expenditure as a percentage of sales. By comparing sales, volume, marketing expense, and margin to past performance and to the performance of competitors, managers can get a partial handle on the return of the portfolio overall. Brand managers already track similar metrics for their brands. The brand portfolio manager tracks these measures for the portfolio, but that's not very different from what we do today.

But not all of the returns to a brand portfolio pop out of management information system (MIS) reports. We don't have well-established and easily tracked benchmarks for trade leverage and competitive advantage. Now this doesn't mean these returns are any less real. A strong brand portfolio, for example, has much greater leverage with a distribution channel than a weaker portfolio. Few consumer electronics retailers like Massachusetts-based Bose Corporation—and no wonder. Bose refuses to fund deep discounting, limits the range it makes available to retailers, sells direct through the mail, and operates its own factory stores. But retailers carry Bose speakers anyway because the brand portfolio is so strong.

That's the intangible side of the return equation for brand portfolios. Channels are more likely to try new products and carry the full range. Suppliers bring new ideas to the strongest portfolio first. Competitors hesitate before launching attacks. Potential alliance partners give more favorable terms. Consumers forgive blunders and even catastrophes more easily. In 1996, an E. coli contamination in Odwalla juices made forty-nine people ill. Odwalla makes natural juices and doesn't pasteurize its products, which would kill the bacteria.[4] But Odwalla recovered from the disaster, in part due to an excellent response and in part due to a strong brand portfolio. In cases like this, the intangible return to the portfolio is as significant as the more tangible ones.

Managing the Risk of Value Erosion

Unfortunately, measuring the risk of a brand portfolio is a more elusive proposition. Brands don't have betas that you can look up on ValueLine.com. Higher levels of risk do show up in the same measures that returns do: weak sales, share loss, and profitability. But by the time metrics like these reveal the true magnitude of problems, it's often too late.

Consider the recent announcement by GM to phase out Oldsmobile. During the last five years, GM spent over $4 billion to fix the Oldsmobile portfolio. Managers pruned weaker brands and launched exciting new extensions such as Aurora. They pumped millions into advertising to reposition the brand with younger consumers. In 1999 alone, GM spent $237 million in advertising to support Oldsmobile, twice the level of 1996. Still, share and sales plummeted. In 1986, Oldsmobile sold over a million cars. In 2000, sales fell to 265,878, and share was half what it had been in 1995.

The problem is less that GM did something wrong and more that it did the right things, but too late. The Oldsmobile turnaround started in the mid-1990s, ten years after problems surfaced and five years after the point of no return. Oldsmobile built its differentiation on the basis of cutting-edge technology—the first assembly line, high-compression engines, front-wheel drive. That reputation for innovative engineering vanished in the late 1980s. And cost-saving tactics like putting Chevrolet engines in Oldsmobile cars blurred differentiation. By the time

GM recognized the risk to the brand portfolio in the mid-1990s, the portfolio was hurtling toward consumer irrelevance.[5]

Peter and Waterman put AT&T, Xerox, Kodak, and Levi Strauss on its list of "excellent companies" in 1981. All are now struggling because of deteriorating brand portfolios. All are now undertaking drastic brand portfolio actions. Xerox has sold its Chinese operations. AT&T has announced plans to split into four different companies—all named AT&T. It may just be too little, too late.

How then can we tell when a portfolio's risk is increasing—before the share graph looks like a ski slope? We can't measure risk very easily, but we can track risk factors. Sub-optimized portfolios show five symptoms that, left untreated, virtually always lead to decreased performance and, over time, value erosion. By watching these indicators, we can track the risk of the brand portfolio and lay out a plan to reduce it.

- *Stagnant growth.* Portfolios should always be growing in pure volume terms. This may seem like a bold statement. But zero-growth or shrinking portfolios are high-risk portfolios. Although it seems hard to believe, every day, somewhere in the marketing world, a manager misses this symptom. Pricing increases disguise volume loss. Marketers explain away losses as a temporary result, one that will soon reverse itself as the economy turns around or as competitors come to their senses. As Oldsmobile learned, it's easy for temporary to turn permanent. Unless you can clearly and unquestionably link the loss of momentum to a one-time event, treat it as a clear sign of risk.

- *Encroachment by competitive portfolios.* Brand portfolios must do more than just grow volume. They can't lose share to competitors. Even if the loss occurs along the edges of the portfolio, it is a sign of risk. Nor does the loss have to be to big, established competitors to be important. The Gaines Division of General Foods was at one time the second largest maker of dog food in the United States. Gaines ignored the threat posed by tiny fringe competitors such as Hill's Science Diet and Iams, instead focusing on the market leader, Purina. Both Hill's and

Iams are now billion-dollar divisions of major consumer products companies, and Gaines no longer exists.

- *Poor resource allocation.* Microeconomists say managers exist to allocate resources. But poor resource allocation doesn't always mean poor managers. Instead it can mean the risk level is rising and managers are stretched trying to cover all the possible flash points with inadequate budgets. What are the telltale signs of resource allocation problems? When marketing budgets become split among too many brand pots, scale efficiencies go down and budget administration costs go up. Inevitably, this leads to conflicts in the brand department. A little jousting is probably a good thing. But there's a point where it stops being healthy competition and turns to frustration. That's a symptom.

- *Nested trademarks.* Trademarks deliver a terrific burst of information to consumers in a very concise, simple package. For example, when Joe Consumer picks up a curved Coke bottle, he knows how the product inside will look, taste, and smell. He knows it will be pure and safe to drink. He may even have an idea of what people will think of him if they see him drinking it. The Coke name and associated iconography deliver all that information in a fraction of a second.

  When Coca-Cola does a promotional bottle, say for the Olympics, the additional logo on the bottle conveys additional information. Exactly what that additional information is depends on the buyer. If he is collector of Coke memorabilia, the four intertwined rings could say, "Buy this bottle, but don't consume it." If he is not a regular Coke drinker but a fan of the Olympics, it could be saying, "Buy this bottle and support your cause." If he is a loyal Coke consumer, it could be reminding him, "We're a world-class company associated with world-class events." Whoever the consumer is, the new logo carries a new burst of information.

  Every additional brand logo or trademark on a product or on an ad says something to someone. Adding more logos can be good or it can be bad. It's good when it brings new consumers into the brand portfolio, or when it increases the stature of the brand. It's bad when it reaches the point of diminishing returns.

Smart marketers get this. Altoids, the tremendously popular breath mint, comes in a distinctive read-and-white tin with three trademarks on the top: Altoids, "The Original Celebrated CURIOUSLY STRONG PEPPERMINTS," and Callard & Bowser. Inside the can, a wrapper mentions Smith & Co., which invented Altoids in 1780. A particularly sharp-eyed consumer could turn the can over and find one more brand in small type at the bottom: Suchard, and from that correctly deduce that Altoids is owned by Callard & Bowser-Suchard, which is owned by Jacobs-Suchard, which is part of Kraft, a division of Philip Morris. Philip Morris and Kraft haven't left their names off the package because they forgot. They know the Kraft logo does not convey persuasive information to the consumer in this case.

When too many trademarks become nested on the product or in the communications, consumers get confused or even angry. Of course, there is no single benchmark for how many is too many. In business-to-consumer markets (B2C), you can often spot excessive nesting just by looking for it. Count the number of different brands or trademarks on a package or ad. For example, we commonly find print advertisements for cars with a half dozen different trademarks. They jump off the page, all yelling to the consumer, "Look at me! No, me!" In business-to-business markets (B2B), when salespeople spend more time explaining how products relate to each other than why the customer should buy them, there may be a nesting problem. Nesting is very easy to detect and a very early sign of risk.

- *Brand portfolio wildfires.* Earlier we spoke about the Audi 5000 ruckus and how it affected the Quattro. There is no shortage of examples of brand portfolio contamination: computer chips in PCs, biotech corn in tortillas, Firestone tires on Ford Explorers.6 Any time brands are connected the risk of a wildfire exists. If wildfires occur frequently, or if there's obvious potential for a wildfire, then the risk level may be getting too high. For example, Johnson & Johnson (J&J) refuses to use its brand on any product that could potentially cause a loss of human life. It doesn't want to risk the portfolio of J&J brands related to infants. If we're going to use brands together to create value, we can't avoid contamination risk. We do need to keep a close eye out.

The Toolkit

We know of eight tools that brand portfolio managers can use to maximize the return and minimize risk. They are (1) extensions, (2) repositioning, (3) pruning, (4) over-branding, (5) co-branding, (6) amalgamation, (7) partitioning, and (8) scaling.

Many executives will find some of these tools familiar, although it's unlikely you will have ever seen them all on a single list before. But don't be deceived. As we've said, using a hammer in space is not the same as using it on the ground. Many marketers are familiar with creating extensions *to* the brand. We're going to talk about how to create extensions *between* brands. And repositioning a portfolio of thirty brands is not quite the same as repositioning a single one.

Also, remember our objectives: higher returns, lower risk. We're going to use these tools in combination: pruning, partitioning, and backfilling to manage risk; extending and amalgamating to improve returns. The net result will be a new way to address brand performance, by working at the brand portfolio level.

7

toolkit:
extensions

It is sometimes necessary to repeat what we all know. All map-makers should place the Mississippi in the same location and avoid originality.
—Saul Bellow, *Mr. Sammler's Planet*

EXTENSION IS THE SIMPLEST, oldest, and most common approach to boosting portfolio returns. It is almost a natural force, because as the research and development (R&D) department develops new technologies and product improvements, brand portfolios grow by extension with or without the guidance of the marketing department. As figure 7-1 for the auto industry illustrates, most new brands are actually extensions. It is a universally popular and often successful brand growth strategy.

Still, brand experts fiercely debate the long-term effects of use and overuse of extensions. Proponents argue that extensions add new volume and greatly increase the efficiency of advertising communications. The statistics show that extensions of already trusted brands will be more successful in the market than will new products or services launched on their own. Launching an extension requires less overall investment. The company does not need to spend millions of marketing dollars to make consumers aware of the new brand. Proponents assert that there is little or no risk if it is done right.[1]

Not everyone agrees. Al and Laura Ries, among others, have long warned about the risks of brand extensions, adamant that extensions generally result in no net gain. The Reises point to American Express, which in 1988 had few brands and 27 percent of the market, and today has fifteen brands and 18 percent share.[2] Some have argued that most extensions are trivial. A survey by Group EFO found 72 percent of product introductions in 1994 could be classified as line extensions. The study found nearly half of those to be "close-in" extensions, new flavors or scents of an established brand in its category. "Line ex-

FIGURE 7-1

Brand Creation by Brand Type: Auto Category, 1993–1994

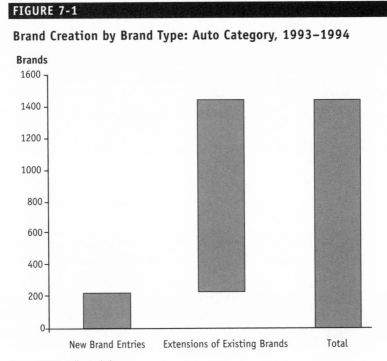

Source: CASSIS, Helios Analysis.

Figure 7-1 is an analysis of new brands that were trademarked in the automotive industry in 1993. *New brand entries* is an estimate of brands that were completely new to the category. *Extensions of existing brands* is an estimate of the brands that were new in 1993, but that were affiliated with a previously introduced brand.

tensions are safer than going into uncharted territory," Mark Wiser, senior director of new products and programs at Arby's and a veteran P&G marketer, told *Brandweek*. "It's easier for managers to rationalize that there is more of a difference to a product than there really is. The consumer sees it as just shades of the same color." According to Group EFO, "the biggest reason products flop is because they have no competitive point of difference, a factor in 73 percent of marketers' most recent failures," *Brandweek* reported.[3]

Even more important, some have argued that extensions are not just a waste of time but dangerous to the core portfolio. Al and Laura Ries have written, "the easiest way to destroy a brand is to put its name on everything" and that "what branding builds, sub-branding [line extensions] destroys." They see the equity of a brand portfolio as a finite quantity. They contend that brand extensions borrow from Peter to pay Paul, a transfer of brand equity from an existing franchise to a new one. If the new extension fails, then that equity has been gambled and lost, resulting in a net dilution to the portfolio. They argue that most extensions merely cannibalize existing business and increase the risk of brand contamination.[4] For example, the Cimarron extension weakened the Cadillac portfolio. Launched in 1980, Cimarron was essentially a Chevrolet Cavalier with leather seats, and a disaster. Twenty years later, Cadillac managers are finding it hard to win over consumers to the excellent Catera, at least in part due to the shadow of Cimarron.[5]

Redefining Extensions

Both camps are clearly right. Extensions do create risk to the portfolio. They have been overused. And they can still create value. The key is to recognize that there are different types of extensions and plot portfolio strategy accordingly. When we say "different types," we not talking about traditional extension classifications like brand, line, and product. We mean that there are extensions within the portfolio and extensions at the edges of the portfolio. They're very different, both in the risk they entail and the potential return.

For less dense portfolios, extension opportunities exist in the open spaces of the molecule. We call these types of extension opportunities *interstitial extensions* because they fill the gaps in the molecule like an interstitial page on the Internet fills the space between content pages. Interstitials are typically lower-risk, higher-probability strategies.

The other type of extension is the *boundary extension.* Boundary extensions are higher-risk, larger-payoff strategies that essentially create new brands on the outer edges of an existing brand molecule. Some of these extensions are relatively stand-alone offerings, while others have a strong connection to the core. The Cimarron was a classic high-risk boundary extension. It was distant from the center of the Cadillac brand portfolio because of its miniature size and mass market price point, but connected enough to cause damage when it failed. The Bose SoundWave radio was a boundary extension that succeeded, as is Virgin Atlantic Airways.

Interstitial Brand Extensions

For leading portfolios, interstitial extensions block competitors and lock in customers with a more compelling and specific offering. For the rest of the pack, they provide a soft spot to attack the leader. We've touched on this example earlier in the book; it's useful to revisit it here: In 1993, P&G's Crest was the number one toothpaste in the United States, with a strong range of toothpastes under the Crest brand. Unilever introduced a baking-soda-and-peroxide toothpaste, Mentadent, which by 1996 had bolted out to $175 million in yearly sales, according to Information Resources Inc., good enough to steal the number three spot in the category from Church & Dwight's Arm & Hammer. Church & Dwight responded almost immediately, and rushed out its own Arm & Hammer Peroxicare within a year of the Mentadent launch.[6]

Crest managers chose not to respond, skeptical that foaming toothpastes had any real therapeutic value. They were right. Mentadent sales later faded. But as they debated, in 1998 Colgate-Palmolive launched an anti-tartar extension, Colgate Total, with the ingredient Triclosan. By 1999, when P&G finally rolled out its Crest entry, Crest Baking Soda & Peroxide-

Whitening with Tartar Protection, it was too late. The Crest brand lost the technological edge to longtime rival Colgate and its number one position for the first time in decades.[7] By the end of 1999, Mentadent had sunk to $136 million in sales. Colgate sat atop the category with sales of $475 million, while overall Crest sales stood at $444 million, approximately the same sales figure P&G racked up in 1994.[8]

This case shows how important interstitials are. For Unilever and Colgate, they provided a way to attack P&G supremacy without pouring more money into advertising head-to-head against Crest. P&G failed to respond rapidly and lost category leadership as a result.

Perhaps P&G was concerned over portfolio clutter—too many extensions. An avalanche of extensions can clog up channels. Or perhaps it was worried about self-cannibalization, an inevitable result of interstitial extension. Why inevitable? In 1994, two researchers looked at 5,474 smokers and the 37 brands they smoked. They carefully analyzed the 188 different brand variations and analyzed the sales of each. They looked at cannibalization of secondary brands by other secondary brands, of secondary brands by primary brands, and of secondary brands by corporate brands on the edge of the portfolio. The study found extensive cannibalization, ranging from 30 percent to 96 percent. The more brands in the portfolio, the higher the levels of cannibalization, in an almost linear relationship.[9]

But better to cannibalize your own brands than to have them successfully attacked by other competitors. Tilex Fresh Shower might take the place of another Tilex stock-keeping unit (SKU) under the bathroom sinks of some consumers, but without it, Clorox would cede an entirely new and growing category to its competitors. For most brand portfolio managers, the cannibalization created by interstitial extensions is an acceptable risk.

And clutter can be managed by partitioning, a tool we will discuss in chapter 13. Partitioning splits a large portfolio into two smaller ones. Our hypothesis is that the limits of manageability will fall at about thirty to fifty brands in a portfolio (or molecule) with no more that a dozen strategic brands.[10] Beyond this, or some similar point, will come clutter and meaning-less extension and needless cannibalization.

Boundary Brand Extensions

But as the data show, most managers are very comfortable with interstitial extensions. They are more interested in how to take the brand beyond the boundaries of the current brand portfolio, to produce undeniably incremental growth by finding new users or entering new categories. For example, look at P&G again, with its licensed extension of its Vicks brand into the appliances business. Via licensee Kaz, Inc., a health care hard-goods maker, P&G now sells Vicks humidifiers, vaporizers, air purifiers, and even inhalers and thermometers. The extensions have moved Vicks into sections of the local Duane Reade or Eckerd where P&G has never been before. Many would consider an extension not truly an extension unless it breaks just such new ground.

Boundary extensions are an exciting way to improve the return, but they are very high risk. Brand portfolios can be expanded in some directions but not others. Brand portfolio boundaries are defined by four factors: technology, consumer segment, distribution channels, and price point (or quality level).

Extending the brand portfolio along the boundaries of consumer segment or technology often works well. Richard Branson, for example, has taken the Virgin brand from record stores into records, airlines, cola, trains, and wedding services, most with considerable success. He has done so because he has been careful to keep every new offering within the overall brand portfolio positioning and personality, appealing to similar sets of customers with a similar youthful, cheeky message. Similarly, Sony has successfully moved from audio and video equipment to its Vaio line of small computers. Just as Branson did, Sony was able to extend its brand portfolio to enter a new segment by leveraging its core technology of miniaturization. Even DE-WALT, a brand of construction tools, has successfully launched a line of heavy-duty radios for construction sites. While the product is different, the core consumer segment and value proposition are the same.

On the other hand, extending the brand portfolio *across* consumer segments, distribution channels, or price points seldom proves successful. In 1990, Holiday Inn decided to launch a new, lower-priced line of hotels. Holiday Inn charges about $75 to $80 a night for its rooms on average, while the rate for the new Holiday Inn Express chain would ring in about $10 less. Unlike its competitors, such as Hilton and Marriott, who market their lower-end lodgings under different brands, Holiday Inn elected to extend the brand portfolio, simply adding "Express" to its primary brand. But consumers didn't get it. They associated the Holiday Inn brand with the higher price point and failed to understand that this was a lower-priced hotel, competitive to the Microtel or Red Roof Inn down the road. Not willing to pay what they expected to be Holiday Inn prices for a quick overnight stay, lodging consumers bypassed the chain. And as of mid-2000, Holiday Inn Express had fallen well short of Holiday Inn's growth expectations for the extension.[11]

Fashion houses like Calvin Klein and Gucci have also crossed segments, channels, and price points and suffered the consequences. Licensees took both brand portfolios into new channels, attempting to reach new customers at a new price point. But instead of the extension expanding the brand's pull and raising its profile, the rest of the brand portfolio was pulled down, a clear erosion of brand equity.

When a portfolio needs to cross price point or product quality boundaries, it's time for a new brand portfolio. When the Gap wanted to cross a price point boundary and participate in a lower-priced line of clothes, it created Old Navy, its hokey, volume retail chain. When Disney wanted to make movies that appealed to a new segment, mature adults, it wisely created an entirely new brand portfolio, Touchstone Pictures.

Both interstitial and boundary extensions can work. Both can help maximize the portfolio. However, regardless of whether the extension is interstitial or boundary, *the positioning of the extension must be consistent with the overall positioning of the portfolio*. If the positioning of the extension is inconsistent, it will, at best, prompt consumers to simply disregard the connection to the brand portfolio and, at worst, taint the overall equity of the portfolio.[12]

Summary

Extension is the oldest and most common approach to brand portfolio maximization. It is very controversial. Critics argue it creates needless complexity, weakens the core brand by diverting resources, and dilutes brand equity. And they are right. But used properly it also blocks competitors and creates new growth opportunities at a reasonably low cost.

One important consideration is to distinguish between the two types of brand extensions. Interstitial extensions are low-risk, low-reward. They fill in holes between the strategic brands in the portfolio. Boundary portfolios are high-risk, high-reward. They are created on the edges of the portfolio, usually to take the portfolio into new market or product segments. Interstitial extensions are very effective in locking in customers and blocking competitors but almost always cannibalize other strategic brands in the portfolio.

Keys to Success

1. Be a first mover or at least a fast responder.

2. Don't clutter the portfolio. If the number of interstitials expands the portfolio beyond fifty brands, look at partitioning (chapter 13).

3. Create boundary extensions along the grain, not across it. You can cut across technologies and products, but never extend across segments, distribution channels, or price points.

4. Stay true to the overall brand promise, that is, make sure the positioning of the extension is consistent with the overall positioning of the portfolio.

Let us emphasize that last point:

When Morgan Stanley merged with Dean Witter, it also acquired Discover, the credit card company. Shortly after the merger, online brokerages began popping up quickly—E*TRADE, Ameritrade, Datek, TD Waterhouse, even Charles

Schwab online. Morgan Stanley Dean Witter felt it needed to compete in this new sector, but its managers worried about cannibalizing their existing Dean Witter base. So the new company launched an online brokerage under the Discover name. It failed. The plain-sense, credit card image of Discover didn't work for online day trading. Soon Dean Witter pulled the service and launched its own branded online brokerage, which fared much better. For Discover, online stock trading was a high-risk boundary extension because it clashed with the positioning of the brand portfolio. For Dean Witter, it was a logical peg in an interstitial hole.

Virgin and Sony have managed to extend their brands very effectively. Where extensions have been less successful, as in Sony's foray into desktop PCs, they have simply been untrue to the accepted spirit and purpose of the core brand. Virgin's line of apparel has struggled, because its initial styles were pricey and somewhat conservative, distinctly at odds with the overall Virgin brand portfolio's hip, value-for-money positioning.[13]

Next to extensions, the most popular tool is probably repositioning, which we will look at next in chapter 8.

8

toolkit: repositioning

Positioning is not about finding what the market wants you to be, but about finding out what you are and owning that space.

 —F. Byron Nahser, *CEO of the Nahser Agency, Chicago, speech at* Adweek's *New Direction Conference, San Francisco, September 24, 1998*

YOU MUST POSITION every new brand in the minds of consumers. A manager must find something new and different about that brand, go into the minds of consumers, and stake out a bit of territory. Whenever a consumer gets thirsty, Coke wants to own that little tiny speck of brain space where the decision between coffee, water, beer, and Pepsi is made. The more brain-space Coke owns, or the more firmly it owns any single territory, the better it has positioned the brand.

Over time, you will have to reposition many brands. There are any number of reasons why. Jean-Noel Kapferer has defined positioning as "the act of relating one facet of a brand to a set of consumer expectations, needs and desires."[1] Perhaps the brand no longer meets consumers' needs or desires. For example, the volume of brown liquors (whiskey, bourbon, scotch) sold in the United States has been dropping for decades. Over the five-year period 1993 to 1998, the share of the leading brown liquor brands fell by 5 percent.[2] Today's consumers just don't enjoy the taste as much as previous generations did. Most of the brands of brown liquor need repositioning to something more relevant to today's consumer.

Kevin Lane Keller sees positioning as making point-of-difference associations, "those that are unique to the brand and are also strongly held and favorable to consumers."[3] Perhaps the brand has lost its unique point of differentiation. The brand isn't bad, it just doesn't stand out from competitors. That's what happened to Winston cigarettes and Michelob beer. They slipped into that nebulous world of the "acceptable brand set," where consumers considered them reasonable purchases, but the brands didn't stand out from the competition.

Perhaps the target market for the brand has aged, and the brand hasn't managed to renew its positioning in the minds of the next generation of consumers, as was the case for Burma Shave and Montgomery Ward. Or perhaps managers see a greater opportunity for the brand if it could reach a greater audience, as Xerox did when it tried to broaden its territory from being the "Copier Company" to the "Document Company."[4] All of these are valid reasons to consider repositioning.

However, repositioning is, if anything, even more challenging than positioning. Positioning requires that consumers learn what a new brand stands for. Repositioning requires that they first unlearn what it no longer stands for. Oldsmobile insisted to consumers that it was "Not your father's Oldsmobile." Few younger consumers were convinced, especially as the company raised the specter of the old "Olds" to sell the new. Absinthe, a drink once blamed for blinding its imbibers, is currently making a comeback in the United Kingdom, to the surprise of those old enough to remember the ban on the drink just prior to World War II. It has taken three generations for the negative associations to fade. Brands face similar dynamics. So it should not surprise us that, for every successful repositioning, such as Marlboro or Andersen

Consulting, there are ten examples—Oldsmobile, Xerox, Sears, Michelob, Miller Lite, Reebok, Nissan, Burger King, boo.com, Pepsi—of failed repositioning attempts.

Repositionings can fail for many reasons—an overreliance on quick-fix advertising instead of addressing more fundamental product performance problems; weak or pompous new positionings; and so forth. But, in our experience, the most common cause of failure is that managers attempt to reposition individual brands independent of the portfolio. Traditional theory argues that positioning, or repositioning, occurs at the individual brand level. In essence, Gillette Mach3 could be repositioned independent of Trac II or Atra, or Bud Lite could be repositioned independent of the flagship Budweiser brand.

We believe the relationships among the brands in a portfolio are critical and that managers must consider them all during any repositioning exercise to give it the best chance of succeeding. As we will see in chapter 15, Miller Brewing Company will not be successful in the repositioning any of its beer lines until it repositions the brand portfolio. GM can continue to spend hundreds of millions promoting Seville STS with a positioning distinct from Cadillac, but it's not going to work. Unless the company repositions the brand portfolio, it is impossible to significantly reposition the individual brands in the portfolio.

Positioning and Repositioning Defined

As figure 8-1 shows, repositioning a brand portfolio requires changing either the target market or the value proposition of the brand portfolio. To change the value proposition, we can try to change the core offering itself—that is, the products or the technology that underlies them, or the brand portfolio's reputation for quality. Or we can try to change the experience around the purchase and use, that is, the personality of the brand portfolio. For example, in the early eighties, Harley-Davidson repositioned its brand to be "the full-sized, classically styled motorcycle for people who see themselves as individuals." To do so, it targeted a new market (affluent baby boomers) and changed virtually every component of the value proposition. It focused the core offering, by abandoning attempts to make smaller, high-tech bikes, improved its reputation for quality, and upgraded customer experience, by refitting dealerships and creating rallies and events. The only thing the company left alone was the portfolio's fundamental personality.

In other cases, a company might choose to focus on the personality. Don Sexton of Columbia University has made an exhaustive (and excellent) study on the repositioning of the Mountain Dew portfolio. Mountain Dew, the ultrasweet, odd-colored lemon-lime drink marketed by Pepsi, is today one of the fastest-growing and most popular products in the carbonated soft drink category in the United States. Throughout Mountain Dew's history, Pepsi has targeted youthful drinkers. But, over time, the company steadily shifted its positioning from hick to hip, with great success. After its creation in the 1960s, early advertising for

FIGURE 8-1

Brand Positioning Framework

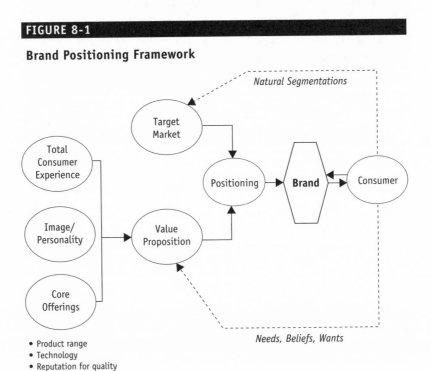

• Product range
• Technology
• Reputation for quality

Figure 8-1 is our framework for thinking about brand positioning. It suggests that brand positioning is a function of a clearly defined target market, and a compelling, differentiated value proposition. Deriving that proposition requires understanding your brand's experience with consumers, its image, and its core product/service specific offerings that are proprietary.

Dew showed a cartoon of a hillbilly with a little brown jug, from which a cork explodes, blowing a hole in his hat. Cue the tag line "Yahoo! Mountain Dew!" At one point, the company offered the product descriptor "Zero-proof hillbilly moonshine."

Over the next thirty years, Mountain Dew consistently moved away from the cornpone imagery. Pepsi gradually incorporated more and more scenes of young people. Ads began to center on outdoor activities, showing healthy, clean-cut teens swinging on a rope and dropping into a river—more contemporary but still fairly hokey in its static young people/summery fun imagery, not unlike Juicy Fruit ads of the time. In the 1990s, however, Pepsi took that youth/active axis and began refining it. Running with the implicit brand asset of Dew's high caffeine content, the company made the brand one of the first to openly leverage a bone-dry Generation X sense of humor, as well as the growing genre of "extreme" sports. Today's ad slogan "Do the Dew" emanates from four funny dudes called the "Dew Crew," whom we find alternatively engaged in such activities as inline skating on the top of skyscrapers and off-road biking to run down a cheetah who has run off with a can of Dew. Supplementing this positioning, Pepsi has also made the brand portfolio a prominent sponsor of ESPN's X-Games, among other "extreme" sports events. Pepsi has made Mountain Dew a sort of clearinghouse for "slacker" culture, offering free rock and rap music downloads, as well as information on sports and entertainment, plus hyperlinks to "cool" Web sites. It is one of the most successful repositionings in marketing history, and one of the fastest, taking only a single generation to accomplish.[5]

Note how Mountain Dew's current evolution goes far deeper than its advertising and tag line. Positioning typically takes decades to move a fraction of an inch. Mountain Dew moved its target market from unaware, conservative youth to those on the edge, and its value proposition from taste to refreshment and, again implicitly, an energy boost.

In the cases of both Harley-Davidson and Mountain Dew these repositionings were successful because they took into account the entire portfolio, not just individual products, and because they used the full range of tactics available to the brand portfolio manager. First, and almost universal to any repositioning, is the launch of a new communications campaign. Second is the development of new products or services intended to signal the new direction of the division, for example, the outrageous Dodge Viper. Third are alliances with companies or brand portfolios whose positioning lies generally where you want to take your own brand portfolio. (We will discuss the third approach in chapter 11.)

An Alternative to Repositioning

Repositioning is the most expensive and highest-risk tool in the brand portfolio manager's toolkit. There are clear limits to what repositionings can and cannot accomplish, and in what time frame. Joseph Schlitz Brewing, in 1975 a $1 billion company coming off 14 percent sales growth for the last year, made a series of operational and legal missteps, most infamously a cost-cutting change in brewing processes that turned out a massive batch of milky beer. The company used its operational savings to undercut competitors on price, compounding its image problems by undermining Schlitz's long-standing premium image. Schlitz attempted to reverse its fortunes with a repositioning, a series of television ads that went its "go for the gusto" ads one better, trotting out ultramacho, buff beer drinkers to reinforce its manly image. At the time, Budweiser and Miller were taking lighter, more humorous approaches—notably Miller Lite's ex-jock, "Taste Great, Less Filling" campaign—and scoring big with them. It was too little, too late. Schlitz's fortunes dwindled until, on June 10, 1982, Stroh Brewing acquired the company, folding Schlitz into a much vaster portfolio, where it fell into obscurity.[6]

An alternative to repositioning, and one with at least as high a success rate, is a return to the portfolio's roots to rejuvenate the positioning. Rather than changing the positioning to reflect a new value proposition or attract a new consumer segment, you simply go back to the original value proposition and original segment with an updated message.

Apple did this by revisiting what had made it such a populist phenomenon in the first place, the small, aesthetically unique PC that didn't require a master's degree to set up and operate. That concept originated with the Macintosh in 1984, and though Apple lost its way in the interim, it managed to breathe new life into it in 1998 with the iMac. In a world of adobe-colored boxes, the egg-shaped, multicolored iMacs stood out like a beacon. And true to iMac's core brand promise, it offered the easiest setup and, most important for the new epoch, easiest online access of any machine on the market. The iMac launch campaign offered up simple print and TV ads, featuring the computers framed lovingly on white backgrounds, with no-nonsense copy addressing the computer's basic benefits. The ads did not have to recast Apple or Macintosh in any way. They merely reminded consumers of the key point of difference of the Macintosh brand all along, now boldly embodied in the sleek new machines. Indeed, the tag line for the iMac was "The Internet computer for the rest of us," a play on the old Macintosh slogan. Kellogg's Corn Flakes, Keds sneakers, Radio Flyer, Jeep, RCA amplifiers, and Kraft Macaroni & Cheese have all had success rejuvenating the brand portfolio.

Rejuvenation is a viable alternative, especially for older brand portfolios with well-entrenched levels of consumer awareness.

Summary

Marlboro went from being an insignificant women's cigarette to a contender for the world's most valuable brand. Andersen Consulting (now Accenture) moved from a little-known appendage of a faceless Big Five accounting firm to one of the largest and hottest consulting firms on the planet. Target became the mass discounter of choice for both the hip and the well-to-do. Repositioning is a uniquely powerful tool.

But repositioning is more challenging than simply positioning. Positioning requires consumers to learn what a brand portfolio stands for. Repositioning requires they first unlearn what it no longer stands for. Of all the tools available to a brand portfolio manager, none comes with a higher risk/reward ratio than repositioning. Three components play a role in a repositioning: a new communications campaign, the launch of new products or services that signal the new direction of the portfolio, and alliances with companies or brand portfolios whose positioning lies close to where you want to take your brand portfolio.

Keys to Success

1. Reposition portfolios, not brands. Look at the brand molecule we drew in chapter 3, and it should be obvious why it is so hard to move a single brand. Moving the mass is easier than trying to fight the portfolio to move a single brand.

2. Be patient. Most of us use the advertising tag line as shorthand when discussing the positioning. Positionings are not tag lines. Tag lines change with great frequency—too great a frequency, typically. Positionings shift with much greater difficulty and, hopefully, care. It typically takes years to reposition a brand portfolio.

3. Use all the tools available to you. Advertising quick fixes are tempting, but rarely successful. Advertising used in combination with new products and alliances stands a much better chance of success.

4. Before taking the high-risk tack of repositioning, make sure you've exhausted the option of revitalizing the brand by taking it back to its roots, à la Apple.

9

toolkit:
pruning

And mothers of large families (who claim to common sense)
Will find a tiger will repay the trouble and expense.
   —Hilaire Belloc, *1896*

IN 1990, several newspapers in Australia and New Zealand ran articles recommending "brand slashing." The story reported a speech by a young American-born consultant living in Sydney. (He is now coauthor of this book.) The consultant recommended cutting brand and product portfolios as a way to control costs and improve business focus. The story netted the consultant a brief notoriety and more than a few invitations to speak at other conferences. And yet only one of his Australian clients ever, in fact, really reduced its brand portfolio in any significant way.[1]

Consultants continue to advocate reducing the number of products and brands via articles with titles like "Brand Consolidation Makes a Lot of Economic Sense."[2]

Companies continue to announce plans to cut brands. Unilever announced early in 2000 that it would pare back to 400 the 1,600 brands in its global portfolio. Then, later in the year, it announced that it would not terminate those 1,200 brands but, rather, allow them to "wither on the vine."[3] Soon after, Unilever acquired SlimFast, Bestfoods, and Ben & Jerry's. The thirty-plus brand variants such as Cherry Garcia and Phish Food will add to the Unilever portfolio. Coupled with the introduction of what one Unilever employee calls a "virtually impossible to count" number of brands launched worldwide in 2000, by the time the "reduction program" is implemented, it will have at best a modest effect. Very few, if any, of these brands will disappear.[4]

Companies hesitate to guillotine brands for very good reasons. Cutting a brand creates an immediate loss of volume. In 2000, DaimlerChrysler announced plans to phase out the Plymouth portfolio of brands, and sales immediately dropped from 165,305 vehicles during the previous year to 83,564. And it's not all that easy to shift that volume to other company brands. Plymouth lost 79,841 vehicles. The Chrysler Group overall was down 78,769 vehicles, suggesting a retention of less than 2 percent.[5]

Many times, cutting brands leaves holes that competitors can exploit. Some years ago, one of us went to the Midwest to help a company address its billowing portfolio of household air fresheners. The number of brand variants was growing exponentially, creating havoc with warehouse productivity and administration costs. Naturally enough, the client asked us why the product range was growing so fast. The answer, simply, was that it took one manager to approve the creation of a new variant, but required the signatures of three vice presidents, those of marketing, sales, and operations, to remove any SKU, roughly the lowest divisible unit of the product hierarchy.

Bureaucracy run amok? Not at all. Smart management. Take, for example, "French Rose," one of the aforementioned company's scents whose sales were concentrated in New Orleans. There, "French Rose" led the pack, and retailers would have howled had the company tried to fold it into one of its many other rose scents. It wasn't just a product, but a brand. By vetoing the deletion, the vice president of sales was protecting valuable competitive turf. Holding onto a niche in this market catered smartly to a strong preference by a significant consumer segment. Taking it out would have left one of those interstitial holes we described in chapter 8. Competitors would have raced to exploit it. The front-line managers were right, and the bean counters were wrong.

Also, even if a brand is not relevant today, it may still prove to be useful in the longer term. For many years, Mountain Dew was a peripheral and trivial brand portfolio for Pepsi. But when the market changed, Mountain Dew became a critical plank in the company strategy.

When to Prune, Where to Prune

And yet brand portfolios need to be pruned. Companies that conscientiously prune brand portfolios tend to grow better.[6] As figure 9-1 shows for the U.S. Auto industry, companies that

FIGURE 9-1

Brand Returns: Auto Industry 1984–1988

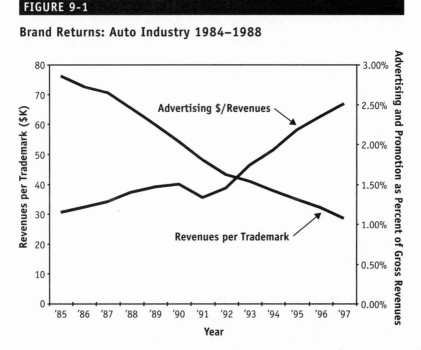

Figure 9-1 is a graphical representation of the comparison between revenues per trademark, and the advertising and promotion costs per trademark in the automotive industry from 1984–1998. The data show an inverse relationship between revenue and cost leading up to the point in 1993 where all new trademarks cost more than they return.

don't prune end up with unmanageable brand portfolios and diluted marketing budgets.

The truth is that brand portfolios are always morphing in aggregate size and shape. Simply slashing brands, simple and clean, is unrealistic in today's hyper-competitive environment. Brand cutting must be thought of differently to be truly relevant today.

First, pruning a brand portfolio should be an iterative process. Managers should prune as often in times of exceptional performance as in times of lagging performance. Brand reductions are almost exclusively announced and attempted in bad times. In 1999, Unilever announced its brand cut plan to save $1.4 billion after consecutive quarters of profit under-performance.[7] P&G, in mid-2000, announced a plan to "focus on its core brands" after faltering earnings growth had pushed its stock price down over 50 percent from its high for the year.[8]

Instead, brand pruning should occur on a periodic basis, for example during every long-term strategic planning process, particularly for more developed brand portfolios. That said, even small portfolio companies should embrace pruning as a proactive tool to keep the portfolio focused on growth areas. During the process, managers should decide which brands or portfolios to prune, and how—cutting or sale? So, pruning should be a proactive tool to manage the brand portfolio. But which brands should remain and which should be pruned?

John Whitney proposed three sets of variables for pruning products and services: significance, profitability, and strategic importance.[9] These variables work for brands as well. P&G recently started paring its $7 billion Beauty Care division. Clearasil, the market-leading acne treatment, was sold first. It was a profitable business but accounted for less than 2 percent of the division's revenues.[10] By cutting Clearasil, a P&G spokesman said, the company could better focus on core brand portfolios like Oil of Olay. Coast soap was also sold so that Safeguard and Zest would benefit.[11] P&G decided to jettison Clearasil and Coast because they were small and insignificant by P&G's standards.

The challenge comes in evaluating brands for strategic importance. We have yet to see a brand that some manager somewhere does not believe is strategically important. And she usually has a good argument and a pound of passion to back up her argument. We have no clean-cut benchmarks for strategic importance. In its plan to cut brands, Unilever said it would keep brands that are number one or number two in their respective markets. "Number one or number two" is implicitly a measure of strategic importance, and a commonly used one. But is it really better to be the number one car-maker in Brazil than number five globally? What if the brand is number three but serves a growing market? What if it is unprofitable but number two? Is number two always OK?

Here is where the BPM can help. By studying the molecule we can visually see which brands are truly strategically important and which are not. For example, say in a typical molecule we immediately see two sets of candidates for elimination: clusters of small, densely packed brands toward the center of the molecule and a cluster of small, isolated, far-flung brands around the perimeter. The brands along the outer edge of the brand molecule are there because they have little relevance to the core of the portfolio. They're too small and too distant to act as silver bullet extensions. Whereas creating extensions in this area is a high-risk proposition, pruning these outer brands is of low risk. These brands are often good candidates for sale.

Thinning the clusters is a tougher proposition. Just as P&G has been making choices between closely comparable brands, like Coast and Safeguard, the marketing manager can make decisions to cut closely related or overlapping brands based on the brand molecule configuration. One obvious caveat: while the brand molecule construct will surface a set of pruning options, managers must at the same time conduct a set of related analyses—for example, of volumetric trade-offs and competitive market restructuring—so that they can make a pruning decision with full information. Nonetheless, densely packed overlapping brands in the molecule offer opportunities to prune at minimal strategic risk.

By using the molecule to determine strategic importance, we remove much of the emotion and subjectivity of strategic importance. We can then discuss strategic importance in the rational terms of risk and reward.

How to Prune

Cutting a brand is no guarantee it will go away. Remember Cimarron? Cadillac customers do. Twenty years later. Brands are remarkably long-lived, resilient organisms. It's hard to kill them unintentionally with bad management, as Harley-Davidson found out in the 1960s. They are even hard to kill deliberately, as Unilever or P&G may soon discover. We ourselves have led consulting engagements that resulted in a long list of brands to be pruned, only to revisit the same client a few years later to find an even longer list of brands. Indeed, often many brands we thought we'd killed still straggled along at the back of the system, grayed and bent over from insufficient R&D, emaciated from lack of marketing support, but indisputably alive.

Packard Bell for years existed as nothing but a discontinued line of TV sets made by Teledyne. In the late 1980s, three entrepreneurs bought rights to the name for $100,000 to use with a new line of PCs to be sold through mass merchandisers. They correctly reasoned that the name alone had the potential to carry their product to high levels of share. The implied, and completely nonexistent, connection to two better-known and respected brand portfolios proved powerful enough to help make the company one of the fastest-growing U.S. PC manufacturers in recent decades.[12]

Best practice seems to be to cut decisively. Allowing brands or portfolios to "wither away" is seldom successful. The costs and liabilities associated with the brand remain, but because it is receiving little or no support, the brand has little chance of success. In a word, all the risks are there of brand contamination, nested trademarks, and poor resource allocation, but none of the rewards. Better to prune and move on.

Where possible, selling the brand or portfolio is a desirable solution if the brand can be cleanly separated from the portfolio. Because P&G has always been careful to create small, stand-alone brand portfolios and has eschewed umbrella brands and nodes to other portfolios, it is able to sell the Clearasil brands relatively easily. Not all portfolios are this lucky. If there is no obvious clean solution, it makes sense to create one. For example, when Andersen Consulting split from Arthur Andersen, it was with the explicit understanding that the new firm would get a new brand name of its own ASAP and not continue to use the Andersen brand. Now Andersen Consulting is Accenture.

Summary

Unilever recently announced plans to slice its global brand portfolio by 75 percent. It remains to be seen if it will be successful. Few brand reduction efforts actually reduce the number of brands in the portfolio. To increase chances of success, managers can prune regularly instead of waiting for a financial crisis to force action. Pruning brands in a portfolio should occur periodically, in times of strong and weak performance alike. Managers can also improve the chances for success by using the brand molecule to decide which brands can be cut at minimal risk. Finally, the brands that are cut should be cleanly severed from the portfolio.

Keys to Success

1. Be decisive. Cut; don't let brands simply atrophy.

2. Choose the brands to be cut carefully. Sure, size and growth-rate are important criteria, but even more important is the role of the brand in the overall system. Pepsi hung onto a relatively minor brand named Mountain Dew because it filled an important hole in the company's range. Today it is the hottest brand in the category.

3. Cut cleanly. Don't leave holdovers or connections to the existing portfolio that will create problems later.

10

toolkit:
over-branding

Turning and turning in the widening gyre
The falcon cannot hear the falconer;
Things fall apart; the center cannot hold;
Mere anarchy is loosed upon the world ...
　—William Butler Yeats, *"The Second Coming"*

As WE WORK WITH CLIENTS we hear no question more often than, "Should we use the corporate name as an umbrella brand?" It is a simple question, but not one that lends itself to a simple answer. Marriott Hotels operates eight different hotel brands: Fairfield, Towne-Place Suites, SpringHill Suites, Courtyard, Residence Inn, Marriott, Renaissance, and Ritz-Carlton. Marriott uses a classic over-branding, or umbrella branding, strategy to optimize the return on its portfolio. The company associates a group of brands with one single brand, Marriott, to gain marketing scale and support the franchise. Each year the company invests $68.3 million in advertising, 76 percent of it behind the umbrella brand.

The Marriott name provides an additional trustmark for lesser-known brands, such as Residence Inn, and is used accordingly. By using the far better known Marriott name, the company also increases the chance of success as it launches and rolls out its newer chains like Courtyard.[1]

When we speak of over-branding, we mean using the brand of the division or company that owns the brand to help make the sale. In practice that means adding a brand on the package, in the advertisements, or on business cards *either in conjunction with or instead of a stand-alone brand*. It doesn't make much difference whether that brand is strictly speaking *over* the other brand, as in MCI Paging, or connected in some other way, as in Friends & Family from MCI. The important thing is that a "bigger" brand steps in, either in lieu of a smaller brand or to help close the deal.

Traditionally, the use of over-brands has been polarized: companies either used them extensively throughout their portfolio or used them sparingly, if at all. General Electric (GE), Sony, AMEX, Microsoft, and 3M have always made the corporate affiliation very visible to the purchaser. For example, GE has GE Aircraft Engines, GE Appliances, GE Capital, GE Lighting, GE Medical Systems, GE Plastics, GE Electrical Distribution and Control, GE Power Systems, GE Information Services, and so forth. The GE brand is used for both B2B products and B2C products, for both products and services.

At the other end of the spectrum is P&G, which uses the Procter & Gamble name very sparingly. You have to have a very good eye to pick out the P&G logo on Charmin, Folgers, Tide, Crest, Prell, Pantene, Pringles, Pampers, Neutrogena, Iams, NyQuil, Always, Cover Girl, Crisco, Tampax, Old Spice, or any of the other P&G brands and brand molecules. Chances are unless you work in the P&G Investor Relations Department, you didn't even know all those brands were part of the P&G company. Many consumer goods companies have followed P&G's lead and been reluctant to over-brand. That said, there are some companies in these consumer packaged goods industries, like Nestlé, that are much stronger advocates and users of over-brands.

To Over-Brand or Not to Over-Brand?

Increasingly, the trend is to work somewhere in between, depending on the situation. Most Fortune 500 companies now have portfolios that display both over-branded and stand-alone brands. For example, the Gap has five major retail chains: Gap, Gap Kids, Baby Gap, Old Navy, and Banana Republic. Before its merger with WorldCom, MCI had MCI Minutes, MCI Personal 800, MCI Paging, MCI Card, MCI Metro, Network MCI, Internet MCI, Friends & Family from MCI, Proof Positive from MCI, 1-800-Collect, and Smart Minutes. This pragmatic approach has taken hold even among companies associated with more extreme positions. P&G has tested the Procter name as an over-brand in some Asian markets; NBC remains NBC, not the GE Television Network; Montgomery Ward never became GE Ward; and Marriott has not laid the parent brand over Ritz-Carlton.

The secret of successful over-branding is linking brands or brand portfolios in ways that make sense to consumers. Consumers understand over-brands that tie together similar brands with similar target markets and value propositions. Groups of brands that live in close proximity are strong candidates for some type of over-branding affiliation. In the Cadillac brand molecule, for example, several line brands exist clustered next to the Cadillac brand: DeVille, Seville, and Escalade. For each of these brands, the Cadillac brand is relatively more important and functions as a meaningful over-brand. Cadillac as an umbrella makes less sense for Catera, which lies at the boundary of the molecule.

Consumers also understand it when a better-known and more trusted brand is placed over a weaker or lesser-known brand. In 1995, AT&T purchased McCaw Cellular and immediately switched the brand for pagers from McCaw to AT&T Wireless. Calls from prospective customers jumped from six hundred a week to six thousand.[2]

However, consumers do not always get the idea of an over-brand, especially a newly created one. In July 2000, AutoNation, the largest new car dealership in the United States, announced that it was discontinuing efforts to establish a national brand for car dealerships. As part of revolutionary vision for the car retailing industry, AutoNation set out on a buying spree in 1996, gobbling up independent car dealerships across the states. After each acquisition, the green highway-style signage of the AutoNation logo was laid as over-brand for the dealership. By the middle of 2000, there were over four hundred AutoNation signs hanging, selling new cars across the states. It seemed straightforward, to buy low-profile branded dealerships and then bundle them together around the AutoNation brand that was receiving tens of millions of dollars in national brand awareness promotions.[3]

But AutoNation failed because the dealer brands held a far stronger franchise with consumers than the company realized. In certain areas of the country, Florida for example, dealer chains like Maroone had built up significant positions with consumers. The Maroone brand actually overshadowed AutoNation's brand in terms of the reasons customers cited for purchasing a particular automobile. The fallout is that in Florida, AutoNation is changing its name at many dealerships, back to Maroone.[4]

Successful Over-Branding

Over-branding, if executed well, can really boost portfolio return and simplify management. The benefits are real and tangible:

1. Over-brands allow economies of scale in advertising. For example, it might cost Marriott twice as much for the same impact if the budget were fragmented among eight different brand portfolios.

2. Over-brands provide an additional trustmark on branded products, especially in categories where existing brands are weak or not well known. For example, Disney has used its brand on cruises. The magazine *Your Company* successfully renamed itself *Fortune Small Business,* using the parent connection to help it stand out from the many

other competitors on the newsstand. In both these examples, the products being over-branded met Disney and Fortune quality standards. If that is not the case, it is very, very dangerous to loan trustmarks. Via licensing, Gucci allowed Gucci to be used as an over-brand on dozens of products in the 1970s. But many of the products with the Gucci over-brand were inferior in quality to the core line. Despite the fact that most of the lower-quality items were sold in very different channels, the brand equity erosion created by out-of-control over-branding nearly sank the company.[5] "Loaning" brand equity is much akin to letting your next-door neighbor drive your Land Rover. You can't control where he goes (and you might not get it back).

3. Over-brands help launch new brands, which inevitably start with low levels of awareness. One of the first online career advancement services, Futurestep, makes a great deal of its parents, especially Korn/Ferry International, the huge executive search firm.

4. And increasingly, given the surge in M&A activity, over-brands cement the integration of companies and signal the change that is to come. The benefits are realized from both organizational and consumer perspectives. First Chicago Bank branches now sport the Bank One logo.

On the other hand—similar to our cautions on cross-boundary extensions—over-branding can increase the portfolio risk to unacceptable levels. Over-branding always increases the risk level—by nesting trademarks and by creating the possibility of brand wildfires. If a new over-brand is created, it can create conflicts over resources. So logically, it makes sense to add risk only when the return justifies it. Just as with extensions, success is most likely when the brands being linked have similar technologies, customer bases, distribution channels, and price points. Marketers should take particular care when using umbrella brands to increase the success rate of new or struggling products.

Summary

Over-brands or umbrellas can provide scale opportunities to subscale portfolios. They make sense when they provide an additional trustmark on branded products in categories where existing brands are weak and when they help launch new products or put them into new geographies. They can be used to facilitate postmerger integration.

But while over-branding may increase portfolio return, it always increases portfolio risk. Over-branding works when it ties together portfolios with similar customer bases, distribution channels, and price points. The litmus test for whether over-branding is appropriate is always the consumer perspective. Since the brand molecule is a snapshot of the consumer's view, it is a useful way to determine whether or not brands are clustered in a way that may allow successful over-branding.

Keys to Success

1. Over-brand for the right reasons.

2. Think like a consumer. No clever and sufficiently broad tag line can tie together two brand portfolios that never should have been linked in the first place. And a contrived over-brand doesn't make management simpler, it makes it more difficult, as the brand portfolio manager spends much of his time trying to force corporate rules on rebellious divisions.

3. Do your homework. Take the time to really understand the differences and similarities between brands. Consider the recent moves by Pegasus in Dallas. In 1989, sixteen hotel and travel-related companies, each with its own separate brand portfolio, founded the company to provide third-party transaction processing for hotel reservations. Over time, it developed three distinct lines of business: The Hotel Industry Switch (THISCO), the Hotel Clearing Corporation (HCC), and Pegasus IQ. It also launched one of the world's first travel Web sites,

TravelWeb.com. In 1999, Pegasus rebranded the three core businesses as Pegasus Electronic Distribution, Pegasus Commission Processing, and Pegasus Business Intelligence.[6] Pegasus spent years carefully thinking through its over-brand before putting it into place.

4. Be conservative. The risks in over-branding are significant. It is better to roll out the over-brand cautiously than to overextend and find yourself with an expensive albatross.

11

toolkit:
co-branding

A good name is to be chosen above great riches.
—Proverbs 22:9

Philips and Levi Strauss recently announced a jacket with built-in electronics—a cell phone hidden in the collar and an MP3 player in the pocket.[1] Caterpillar boots, Jeep radios, Camel watches, Nickelodeon toys, Eddie Bauer Ford Explorers, Delta Airlines Optima cards, Starbucks and Godiva ice creams by Dreyers, soft-drinks from Coke and Disney, Vicks humidifiers by Kaz—all are combinations of brands that create value. Co-branding is a way of using the brand portfolios of others to reach new markets and create new businesses. In the process, you can tap the expertise of other manufacturers and marketers to reduce your own risk of portfolio boundary extensions.

To be clear, when we talk of co-branding and brand portfolio alliances, we are defining the terms in their broadest sense. This includes actual paired names like Citibank Visa. And we're including brands that go to market side by side without changing names, like Barnes & Noble and Starbucks—the same brand names, but seen together inside the bookstores. It can even include original equipment manufacturer (OEM) agreements where one brand is recognized only through its product shape or character, as when Compaq provides its printers to be branded and sold by Lexmark. It includes substantive Web site links and marketing promotions. When those alliances are intended to be long lasting and visible to consumers, we term them co-brands.

Brand partnering is relatively new, but that hasn't stopped it from becoming one of the most popular tools around. Every executive must now deal with alliances, associate programs, licensing, and joint marketing agreements. In the mid-1980s, only one in ten U.S. companies sought out intercorporate alliances to extend its brands.[2] Now 65 percent are partners in such deals. For years, GM tried to track down and stamp out trademark infringers. The company spent millions of dollars every year hunting small print shops that were turning out bumper stickers with the distinctive Chevy logo. Now the corporation boasts more than 1,200 licensing agreements generating annual revenues of over a billion dollars. The Sunkist grower's co-op made more than $10 million for licensing its name into such alliances in the 1980s alone.[3] The use of click-throughs on Web pages has created a whole new category of alliances and partnerships.

Some partnerships are temporary. In the mid-1990s, J&J poured its famous No Tears baby shampoo into a series of bottles shaped like characters from Winnie-the-Pooh. It was deliberately short-term. They sold like gangbusters—an alliance of two very successful brands to create something new and special. Some partnerships, on the other hand, are long lasting—two companies which together create a new virtual brand. Nike and the NBA have built their brands together so closely linked that they have at times appeared components of a single portfolio. Kmart sells varied lines of Martha Stewart products, including a new set of garden tools. Regardless of the mechanics, co-branding offers a powerful tool to up the return on the brand portfolio.

Alliances and Co-Branding

Linking your brand portfolio to one owned by another company—no matter how you do it—can create a bridge to new growth areas. John Deere's three-way alliance with Scott's and The Home Depot is a case in point.

John Deere, the manufacturer of agricultural and construction equipment, succeeds in tough cyclical markets where competitors come and go. What sets John Deere apart is less its engineering than its brand portfolio, built with a marketing acumen rare in heavy industrial businesses. Many consumers with little or no connection to the agricultural base know John Deere green, the running deer icon, and the company's slogan, "Nothing runs like a Deere."

Using this latent consumer awareness, John Deere built a $2.6 billion business in lawn care equipment, making the unit larger than its construction equipment division and almost half as large as its mighty agricultural equipment division. A key element of the company's growth was the launch of a John Deere riding mower or "lawn tractor" that looks just like the John Deere agricultural tractor. (The popular 1999 movie *The Straight Story* recounts the tale of an elderly man, Alvin Straight, who drove his riding mower almost four hundred miles from Iowa to Wisconsin to see his ailing, estranged brother. In it, we witness a wonderful scene of Straight riding down a dirt road on his John Deere lawn tractor side by side with a farmer on a towering agricultural tractor. The resemblance is uncanny and deliberate.)

Originally the lawn tractors were sold only through John Deere agricultural equipment dealers. Then the company started marketing them through carefully selected lawn mower specialty outlets. They were very successful. But when John Deere wanted to reach a broader consumer market, it joined a three-way alliance to create the "Scott's from John Deere" riding mower for The Home Depot. And it did it the right way. The company did not simply stamp the primary John Deere brand on a product bound for the mass merchandiser channel, which would have alienated dealers, created control problems with pricing and perhaps made those miniature John Deere tractors seem not quite so special. The Scott's lawn tractor is green, but not Deere green. John Deere has used an alliance to extend its portfolio into a new consumer segment as well as into a new channel.

When Alliances Work

Alliances work when the portfolios have similar values and positionings. Your grandmother was right: You are known by the company that you keep. So are brand portfolios. Research has shown that consumers ignore brand extensions that do not make intuitive sense.[4] Similarly, they recognize alliances that reflect intuitive logic and ignore those that do not. For J&J, the Winnie-the-Pooh linkup was a natural. Rather than trying to create its own line of lovable figures, J&J capitalized on the equity already established by author A. A. Milne over decades and popularized in Disney films. The two brand portfolios share similar value propositions, personalities, and gestalt.

Contrast that pairing with another clearly contrived alliance that did not work. A decade ago, the U.K. retailer Sainsbury struck an elaborate and extended deal whereby customers got free flights on British Airways. Justifying the alliance, a spokesman explained hopefully, "It's the world's favorite airline and Britain's favorite supermarket."[5]

You need to be careful to consider just how much control you're vesting in your new partner. Ask yourself if you're sure that you share a common purpose and direction? Alliances work when there is commonality of purpose and fail when there is not. In May 2000, Calvin Klein filed a lawsuit against Warnaco, manufacturer of jeans under the Calvin Klein label, and owner of the CK underwear brand. It charged Warnaco with diluting the CK trademark by selling into discount channels. For example, Warnaco had recently announced plans to sell CK underwear in J. C. Penney stores, a move that prompted the more upscale Dillard's and Federated Department Stores to announce plans to reduce or end future orders. "We simply cannot stand by and jeopardize the integrity and value of our trademark," Klein said. He claimed that the CEO of Warnaco, Linda Wachner, gave his company repeated promises that she would act as a "careful custodian of the CK brand" but failed to do so.[6]

For Calvin Klein, the real story began in 1994, when, after a brush with bankruptcy, Klein sold the CK underwear business to Warnaco to raise cash. Soon he struck another licensing deal with the company to manufacture and distribute his jeanswear brands. This arrangement runs through 2034. While the deal allows for Klein's input on marketing decisions, Warnaco retains control of this aspect of the brand system on a day-to-day basis. At first, it seemed the Klein people were delighted with the arrangement. According to published reports, Warnaco quickly built the underwear brand from $50 million to $340 million and took care of all the details, so much so that Klein did not even attend design meetings for months at a time. But when Klein tried to sell his company in late 1999, he quickly found little investor interest in a brand-centric company that did not control its own brands. Klein blamed the failure on suspect management decisions by his licensing partner and has filed a lawsuit calling Warnaco a "cancer on the value and integrity of the brand."[7] The alliance failed because the objectives of the two partners diverged sharply over time.

Finally, it's worth looking at what each side is bringing to the party—is each partner making a unique contribution? When Bose began making stereos for Cadillac, it worked because Cadillac's customer base married well with Bose's technology and brand. The coupling of Neiman Marcus and BMW for the retailer's rewards program seems a neat demographic fit as well.

The idea of unique contribution is important. That is, the brand portfolios can share *too much* in common. In the early 1990s, Fisher Price and McDonald's created an alliance to produce a line of play food and appliances for children. It was unsuccessful. The problem wasn't that each partner didn't bring something to the party, but rather that they both brought the same thing.[8]

Managing the Risk

Co-branding can be used as a tool to help reduce brand portfolio risk, especially by lowering the risk of failure of boundary extensions. But it also creates a set of risks as well. There are the risks of an expensive failure or of a falling out with partners, and there is the risk of brand contamination. Any one of them can result in very serious brand equity erosion, if you don't keep them in check.

Calvin Klein was not the first or only fashion house to go the licensing route. In the late 1970s, the big fashion houses were among the first to grasp the opportunites presented by co-branding and alliances. By loaning their brand to companies that could produce high-volume goods for the mass market, they reaped 5 to 10 percent licensing fees with minimal effort or expenditure. And, the logic ran, since the haute couture market and the mass retailers served completely different consumer segments, they ran little risk of erosion of brand equity. Gucci, Dior, Yves St. Laurent, and Givenchy all signed extensive licensing arrangements.

As it turned out, Gucci almost collapsed, and only drastic restructuring, cost cutting, and aggressive brand rebuilding saved it. Today, these companies still struggle to wriggle free of their licensing deals.

There is also a more subtle strategic risk: loss of control of the brand portfolio. In April 1999, McDonald's began a search for a new marketing chief. A number of top-tier marketing all-stars, from Visa to Sears to Young & Rubicam, turned down the position. *Brandweek* reported that many potential candidates felt reluctant to take a job in which McDonald's "Walt Disney alliance puts the studio in the driver's seat on national promotions." One *Brandweek* source summed it up: "Disney is driving their marketing."[9] The perception was that Disney, not McDonald's, controlled key elements of McDonald's marketing.

It is important to evaluate each and every alliance not just for potential return, but also for risk. Temporary alliances should be evaluated for complementarity of positionings and relative contribution. More permanent co-branding relationships should be very carefully scrutinized for commonality of purpose.

Summary

Linking brand portfolios can create bridges to dynamic new growth areas. It can reduce the risk of boundary brand extensions and put unused brand equity to work. Often the risk is more manageable than with other tools.

Co-brands, leveraged well, can help bring a brand to your target consumers in ways not afforded by the immediate business of your current portfolio. A clear and obvious complementarity between brand portfolios with similar, but not identical, positionings can spin fresh points of relevance and context for your brand in consumers' eyes. The payoff comes not only in new volume but, in cases like John Deere, in a whole new set of opportunities for the brand portfolio.

Keys to Success

1. Effective matchmaking. Specifically, brand portfolios should overlap but not occupy identical positionings, and there should be commonality of purpose as well. Co-branding will affect the positionings of both portfolios. Make sure that both portfolios have clearly stated objectives and guidelines and that the co-brand delivers.

2. Keep the messaging simple. The joint message should be clear and intuitively obvious. Look, for example, at "Worldnet from AT&T powered by Lycos," from the Internet service provider arena. It takes quite a bit of deciphering to deduce exactly what the combined proposition is. Disney toys at McDonald's. Got it. Bacardi and Coke. Got it.

3. Get what you pay for. Co-branding increases risk. Make sure the return is worth it. The co-branding relationship should reflect the underlying business logic. Understand who is creating the value and share it appropriately.

4. Manage risks proactively. Remember, any time portfolios
   are linked, it creates a new set of risks. Sit down with the
   brand portfolio guidelines and brand molecules and really
   scrutinize every potential alliance. Put very careful and
   explicit guidelines in place about what is and is not OK.
   As the Disney case of instituting tighter controls indicates
   (chapter 2), the better spelled-out the guidelines are, the
   better the results.

12

toolkit: amalgamation

The great artist is the simplifier.
—Henri-Frédéric Ameil, *Private Journal, 1861*

I N THE WAKE of British Petroleum's (BP) merger with Amoco, BP announced plans to spend $200 million making over all of its 29,000 stations worldwide, rebranding all Amoco stations as BP. The Amoco brand will live on only as a portion of the corporate name and as a stand-alone product line inside larger BP stations (and in consumers' memories).[1] Over time, we can reasonably expect the Amoco name to atrophy and disappear.

When companies amalgamate brand portfolios, they often eliminate one or more of the existing brand names in the process. Upon taking over First Chicago NBD, Bank One wasted no time in replacing the brand. When United Airlines bought PanAm's Pacific route network in 1986, some of the PanAm planes landed at United's huge San Francisco maintenance facility, were wheeled into a hangar, quickly repainted, and wheeled out, paint still damp, for flights to Korea and Taiwan.

In each situation above, amalgamation was the result of a merger or an acquisition. That's a natural time to consider amalgamation opportunities. However, amalgamations are not only for sorting out mergers. Consider NBC's online presence, built by merger, acquisition, and amalgamation. NBC combined brands effectively to create a strong position online. NBC.com was late to the portal party in 1998 but caught up by amalgamating a set of portals into the NBCi.com site. NBCi was launched in November 1999 through the combination of NBC.com and CNET's Snap.com, Xoom.com, NBC Interactive Neighborhood, VideoSeeker, and a 10 percent equity stake in CNBC.com. The amalgamation bumped unique visitors up by over five million.[2]

When you do it correctly, amalgamation creates a bigger brand and reduces portfolio clutter. BP, which has to manage three brands of retail outlets—BP, Amoco, and ARCO—has now simplified it to two retail brands (BP and ARCO). Ideally, this should give BP increased scale in communications and product development. And by cleverly separating the retail brand from the product brands available in the outlets and keeping the Amoco product name in another form, BP hopes to avoid losing the equity associated with that product line.

Fortune Favors the Bold

Amalgamation is one of the most powerful brand portfolio tools because it renders the complex more simple, and allows a company to concentrate its marketing resources. Unilever has announced plans to change the name of the best-selling household cleanser in Britain from Jif to Cif, as it is known in other countries. Unilever is betting that the long-term advantages of managing fewer brand names will more than make up for the costs of the changeover. Also in Britain, Mars renamed its Marathon candy bar to Snickers to bring it into alignment with the name used in other countries.[3] And Nestlé has used amalgamation wisely in building what are ten arguably global brands: Nestlé, Carnation, Buitoni, Maggi, Perrier, Nescafé, Nestea, Libby's, Friskies, and Nestlé Food Services.[4] Most of these brands have been boosted at some point in time by amalgamating a strong local or national brand into a Nestlé division. For example, Nestlé completely replaced the Cambourcy brand on dairy products to build a foothold in France.

Amalgamation is a solution that allows brand portfolio managers far more control than alternative solutions, such as over-branding. With over-branding, there's always the risk of confusing consumers with the sheer number of brand names on a product's package, and the multiple messages being sent by all those brands. With amalgamation, the brand portfolio manager picks and chooses which brands the consumer sees on the package, and which brands she will support with advertising and other resources. Amalgamation also often provides the necessary catalyst for further portfolio pruning.

However, amalgamation is not for the faint-hearted. Consider the case of Amoco. Experts have long regarded Amoco as one of the best brand names in the gasoline industry. Despite the commodity nature of the industry, analysis after analysis suggests that Amoco gasolines command a small premium over other manufacturer's products. For BP, retiring the Amoco name involves considerable risk of consumer and distribution channel backlash. It could not have been an easy decision.

Amalgamation is also costly. Hugh McColl, the CEO of NationsBank, for years proclaimed that the Bank of America brand name had more potential than any other in the banking industry. In fact, he chose the name NationsBank in part as homage to Bank of America. When NationsBank and Bank of America merged in September 1997, the new entity rushed to amalgamate the brand portfolios, and replace the NationsBank brand with that of Bank of America. Six months later, Torod Neptune, a bank spokesman, professed that managers were still trying to get their hands around how much it would cost and how long it would take to replace the 45,000 jointly owned signs across the country and other outdated logoed items. Texas was estimated to cost $5 million alone.[5] Executives originally estimated the change would take twelve to eighteen months but have now doubled that estimate.

Making It Work

It's a tricky shell game deciding which brand to replace and when. The objective should be to create the maximum simplicity with the minimum volume and share loss. Doing so requires a deep understanding of the brand portfolio in question. For example, many foods have strong emotional and cultural identifications. In Australia, Kraft owns the Vegemite brand, one that virtually stands for the country to many Australians and visitors. We hope, for example, that the Kraft will never consider amalgamating its Vegemite brand into another...at least in Australia.

We think the best way to start is with the brand portfolio molecules of the two portfolios under consideration. Map both brand portfolios and identify overlaps and empty spaces. Examine the breadth of both portfolios. See if the target markets are the same.

Then calculate the potential savings to be gained by amalgamation. In our experience, amalgamation offers three significant areas of return. The first and most obvious is scale economies in marketing. Advertising is the most scale-sensitive line on the profit and loss sheet (P&L). A Super Bowl ad costs $2 million whether you have $10 million in sales or $10 billion. But the per unit cost is much lower for the larger company. Amalgamating brands can allow concentration of advertising dollars in a more efficient way. Companies often find similar savings in administration—keeping only one Web site, updating one set of stationery, and so on. Less easily calculated are the advantages gained from increased organizational focus. But these can be even more significant. As the Zebra Technologies case in chapter 5 showed, managing multiple brand portfolios takes effort.

The biggest potential costs of amalgamation will be the loss of volume and share, just as in the case of pruning. To minimize the risk, most companies choose a gradual phasing out of the lesser brands. PricewaterhouseCoopers (PwC), a leading professional services firm, has changed its brand name almost every decade for the last century and a half, making it longer for a short period following an acquisition or merger, then gradually amalgamating back down again over time. The Price and Waterhouse arms of the business started in 1849 with Samuel Lowell Price. Price merged with another firm to become Price, Holyland and Waterhouse in 1865, which next became Price Waterhouse & Co., and then Price Waterhouse World Firm in 1882. The Cooper part began in London with William Cooper in 1854, which became Cooper Brothers. Robert H. Montgomery, William M. Lybrand, Adam A. Ross Jr., and his brother T. Edward Ross formed Lybrand, Ross Brothers and Montgomery in 1898. Cooper Brothers & Co, McDonald, Currie and Co, and Lybrand, Ross Bros & Montgomery merged to form Coopers & Lybrand in 1957. In 1998, the worldwide merger of Price Waterhouse and Coopers & Lybrand created PricewaterhouseCoopers.[6]

For package goods companies, this gradual phasing out takes the form of using both names simultaneously on the package and over time phasing the older brand out. The font on the disappearing name gets smaller and fainter, until at last it just disappears. However untidy this solution, it probably makes sense unless, like BP, you have a $200 million ad budget to work with.

Summary

Amalgamation consists of merging two brand portfolios and eliminating one or more of the existing brand names in the process. It is one of the most powerful tools for managing the brand portfolio. Companies can use it to accelerate the benefits of M&A, and a well-planned strategy of amalgamation can build a strong brand portfolio quickly. When companies do it well, the costs of marketing and administration fall, and the improved focus on the business drives the top line.

But amalgamation requires boldness. Amalgamation costs money. Done poorly, it can result in volume loss and share erosion, and it can distract the organization. Of all the moves to the brand portfolio, amalgamation is the most difficult to reverse. Therefore amalgamation requires very careful planning.

Keys to Success

1. No shotgun marriages. Not all brand portfolios belong together.

2. Choose the amalgamated brand wisely. In 1987, after United Airlines CEO Richard Ferris spent $2.3 billion to buy up Hilton hotels and Hertz Rent A Car, the company made the decision to rebrand as Allegis. Ferris hoped to establish a master brand travel powerhouse. A 1988 survey found that, in terms of name recognition and "esteem" that consumers afforded brands, Allegis ranked in the bottom 5 percent of corporate identities. United, meanwhile, still scored in the top 15 percent in awareness and the top 10 percent in consumer esteem. Ferris was gone a year after taking the helm, and fourteen months after it became Allegis, United flew again, a 360-degree turn that cost the company $8 million in marketing and collateral expenditures, such as repainting its fleet *twice*.[7]

3. Have a clear plan. In 1998, Sierra Inc., a software company owned by Cendant Software, decided to rebrand to bring together the many independent software groups it owns. These include Berkeley Portfolios, Dynamix, Yosemite Entertainment, Papyrus, Front Page Sports, Impressions, and Pyrotechnix. In addition, Sierra owns literally dozens of individual game titles such as Red Baron 2, Blood of the Damned, Golf Pro 99, and others (many of them acquisitions). To unify this disparate portfolio, Sierra decided to create a brand family with six divisions—Sierra Studios, Sierra FX, Sierra Attractions, and so

on.[8] Over time the Sierra brand will replace the many brands underneath, leaving an orderly and hopefully manageable brand portfolio.

4. Ruthlessly rationalize superfluous brands. When brand portfolios are combined, *something* should fall by the wayside.

5. But do so deliberately.

13

toolkit:
partitioning

I would not give a fig for the simplicity this side of complexity,
but I would give my life for the simplicity on the other side of
complexity.
    —Judge Oliver Wendell Holmes

O VER TIME, brand portfolios grow. It's the nature of the game. But with growth comes density, and an increase in the number of brands at the "edge" of a BPM. Sometimes those brands—often the newer entries—fit comfortably as part of the molecule, and add to the overall power of the portfolio. But often, they don't add much, if any, value. And sometimes they link with other, nearby brands, to form a "mini-molecule" of sorts whose positioning is in fact at odds with that of the overall portfolio. These brands may use different technologies than the brands that make up the core of the molecule; or they might have different customer bases. At any rate, when you find that your portfolio has become very diverse, or when your portfolio has grown to the point of being cumbersome, it's probably time to consider partitioning: separating a brand portfolio into two or more unique portfolios.

Financially and Operationally Driven Partitioning

Partitioning is often successful because it makes possible far greater focus. Consider the amicable split up of HP and Agilent. Hewlett-Packard was founded in 1939 in a garage in Palo Alto, California, as a maker of scientific instruments. Over the next sixty years, the company grew to become the fourteenth largest company on the Fortune 500, a $47 billion behemoth with 124,600 employees in 120 countries. In addition to making test and measurement equipment, it had come to make products such as fiber-optic transceivers, health care diagnostic machines, and chemical analysis equipment. But that was not all. HP along the way became the largest maker of computer printers, the second largest maker of PCs that sell at retail, and a huge supplier of workstations, servers, and software.

In November 1999, HP spun off from Agilent. Agilent took with it the more technical, laboratory-oriented product lines, while HP kept those associated with the computer business. The split allowed HP's new CEO, Carly Fiorina, to focus on printers, computer technology, and Internet portfolios, where HP's growth lagged behind more focused brands such as Sun Microsystems.[1] As soon as they announced the split, both HP and Agilent launched major new communications campaigns to put some space between the brand portfolios, although Agilent couldn't quite break the emotional bond.[2] Its tag line reads, "Innovating the HP Way."[3]

The HP/Agilent split was, like many such megapartitions, financially and operationally driven. Nonetheless, from a brand portfolio perspective, there was substantial rationale for the move. Over the decades, the HP brand had developed into four distinct portfolios: communications, electronics, health care, and life sciences. The brand density in each of those areas was huge at the time spin-off occurred. Each portfolio contained hundreds of offerings. By partitioning, both companies feel they will be better able to focus on their markets.

The financial markets agreed. On November 18, 1999, Agilent's first day of trading, its shares shot up 47 percent to $44, while HP, in its next fiscal quarter after the spin-off, ended April 30, 2000, saw its revenues grow 17 percent over that quarter the previous year. The next August, HP's board approved a two-for-one stock split.[4]

Financially driven partitioning (with an underlying logic in operations) has become common. Most brand portfolio partitioning is financially driven. Usually, top management decides that the firm is undervalued because its range of businesses has become sufficiently broad that the market is confused. Typically, the company spins off its lower-margin, more "commodity businesses," as recently happened when Novartis and Zeneca, two large pharmaceutical companies, decided to spin off their agribusiness division as a new company named Syngenta.[5]

When a Zeneca splits from an ICI, or a Lucent from an AT&T, or a 3Com from a Palm, or an Alliant from a Kraft, or a Tricon from a PepsiCo, both brand portfolios typically prosper. Gains in focus and autonomy typically outweigh any losses from reduced scale. A McKinsey & Company study found that straight spin-offs gained an average of 27 percent annually during their first two years as public companies, with the bulk of those gains from small-cap rather than large-cap (large capitalization) companies. By contrast, carve-outs (like a spin-off, but the parent company keeps a big piece of the equity) delivered a 24 percent annualized return. Similarly, a J. P. Morgan study that examined 231 spin-offs and carve-outs between 1985 and 1998 found that during their first 18 months of trading, straight spin-offs beat the Standard & Poor's 500 stock index by 11.3 percent versus 10.1 percent for carve-outs.[6]

But partioning for primarily operational reasons, makes sense as well. Consider the professional services industry. Ernst & Young sold its consulting business to Cap Gemini; PwC spun off its Human Resources, e-commerce practice to form Unifi.com. And after spending hundreds of millions of dollars building its brand, Andersen Consulting must now, as part of an ugly managerial negotiation, leave its name behind for its auditing counterparts as part of its spin-off from Arthur Andersen.[7]

Brand Portfolio Partitioning

The examples we've discussed show that partitioning on a major scale—spinning off new companies, whether wholly or in part—can really give groups of brands the room and attention they need to flourish. But not all partitionings need to be so extreme. Companies can also partition to improve the performance of their brand portfolios. Brand portfolio partitioning does not so much require the company sell off the brand as simply to split the portfolio apart and give the new portfolio its own name and resources.

Black & Decker began making power tools in 1916, and built a reputation for quality and innovation. But in the 1980s Black & Decker re-focused on the home market, making $29.99 power drills and circular saws, as well as small appliances such as the Dustbuster. As a result, it completely lost its position in the professional tradesman market segment, losing share to high-end imports such as Makita. By 1990, market share had fallen to below 10 percent. The views of one professional carpenter summed up the problem: "Black and Decker makes a good popcorn popper and my wife loves her Dustbuster, but I'm out here trying to make a living.... If I came out here with a Black and Decker ... I'd be laughed at." Then, in 1992 Black & Decker re-launched its professional tool line as DeWALT. The newly separated brand portfolio has grown to almost $1 billion, nearly 20 percent of Black & Decker's $4.9 billion sales in 1997.[8] DeWALT now has a 45 percent share of the market.

Levi provides another success story. The company failed in stretching its brand portfolio to cover casual suits. But when it partitioned the portfolio and created Dockers and Slates, it had instant success: 75 percent of American men own a pair of Dockers.[9] Again, partitioning dramatically increased the return on the brand portfolio. Companies can also use partitioning to reduce risks. If Dockers had failed, the Levi portfolio would not have felt the backlash.

If anything, partitioning is an underutilized tool. Yes, loss of marketing scale is an issue. However, portfolios that are really ripe for partitioning may have less scale than at first appears. For example, consider the HP example. Despite HP's huge consumer advertising budget, it still must advertise its scientific products in specialist publications that reach a very specific audience. And those products need their own product manager who understands that particular market. Partitioning won't have an appreciable effect on driving up marketing costs.

Companies also use partitioning to manage risks. When the primary brand becomes so large and prominent that it invites attack by either competitors or third parties, such as regulators and activists, partitioning can be a useful tool. Look at Providian, a successful San Francisco-based bank that operates in subprime lending, a category that frequently gets the attention of zealous regulators and consumer advocates. In 1999, Providian was forced to set aside over $300 million to repay California customers who allegedly had been fooled into buying products they did not want by aggressive Providian telemarketers. The company still faces lawsuits in other states and in federal court.[10]

It all began in June of 1999, when Providian Financial found itself the target of an investigative reporter in San Francisco. Despite furious protests and an active public relations defense by Providian, consumer groups and regulators in several states quickly piled on. Although the number of complaints represents an extraordinarily small proportion of the company's customer base, the sheer size and prominence of the Providian brand served as a lightning rod. Soon Providian became the subject of daily, negative coverage in newspapers across several states.

Without commenting on the validity of the suit, we should note that the entire fracas began as result of the work of a single crusading journalist on a single paper. A single journalist. No huge mountain of complaints was piling up in the California District Attorney's office. Just the opposite: One could measure the number of dissatisfied Providian customers in fractions of a percent. But with a single, monolithic brand, the company made itself naturally vulnerable to brand portfolio contamination. Had Providian had a less concentrated brand portfolio, perhaps the damage could have been contained behind a brand firewall, say, one *other*-branded operating unit, rather than spreading like a New Mexico forest fire across the entire portfolio.

The secret to partitioning lies in understanding the breadth and limits of your brand portfolio. The starting point of course is the molecule. When portfolios become too large, say over fifty brands, or when they become very diverse, it's time to consider partitioning. When the portfolio is very positive from the perspective of one consumer segment, but very negative from that of another highly desirable segment, it's time to consider partitioning. When marketing messages are getting compromised or homogenized because another business unit serving another segment is concerned over the repercussions on its business, it's time to consider partitioning.

Summary

Over time, brand portfolios grow and there comes a point when their size and breadth become dysfunctional.[11] Either they are just so large that management becomes unwieldy, or every decision becomes a compromise because of conflicting priorities. When that time comes, it's time to partition. Brand portfolio managers are often naturally reluctant to partition, concerned that costs will rise as scale is lost. Learn a lesson from financially driven partitioning: The benefits of focus often outweigh the lost scale.

Keys to Success

1. Think like a consumer. If the different consumer segments are starting to become confused, consider partitioning. Early is better than late.

2. Don't emulate Solomon. In the Bible, Solomon settled a dispute between two women fighting over a baby by offering to cut the child in half. Often brand partitionings end up with portfolios cut in half. For example, in 1994, GE sold its home appliance business, with its GE name, to Black & Decker.[12] AT&T announced a partitioning whereby four different businesses will each be called AT&T. Longer term, this type of partitioning can lead to

real problems, for example, brand portfolio contamination. Give one of the new portfolios a new name.

3. Create some distance between the two portfolios. Do as HP did, moving not just the Agilent portfolio away from HP, but the HP portfolio away from Agilent.

14

toolkit: scaling

*An idea that is not dangerous is unworthy of being called an
idea at all.*
—Elbert Hubbard. *Roycroft Dictionary, 1923*

LEVI STRAUSS is the world's leading maker of brand
name clothing. Still. But since 1996, Levi's sales have
fallen more than 15 percent, by over $1 billion.[1] The
reason? The brand has not been able to maintain a majority share in the wardrobes of the baggy-jean wearing
teens of America. Levi has not done anything wrong to
cause the decline, but rather the market has moved out
from under its proverbial feet and the company has not
been able to keep up.

All markets move, or to be more correct, segment.
The middle market, for instance, becomes three markets—low-middle, middle-middle, and high-middle, as
it has in the retail industry, leaving companies like

Montgomery Ward besieged by Kmart and The Home Depot at one end and Nordstrom's at the other. Tomorrow, every one of these segments will divide again, and again.

The premium market becomes premium and superpremium. In the 1960s, Smirnoff was the high-end vodka, with slick advertisements in leading magazines showing Woody Allen entertaining his friends at "Smirnoff Mule" parties. In the 1980s and 1990s, Absolut became the vodka of choice. Today, Smirnoff is no longer trendy, and Absolut executives worry as bartenders in hip nightspots take Absolut bottles down from the shelves behind the bar and replace them with Grey Goose and Ketel One.[2]

The challenge for brand portfolios is how to respond. Follow the market upscale and sacrifice volume? Go downmarket and risk pricing erosion? Or try to span the separating segments with broader brand portfolio extensions, as Mercedes-Benz has tried to do with its C series?

Scaling

Brand portfolios seldom succeed in spanning moving markets. At best, the portfolio ends up firmly in one camp or the other. At worst, the portfolio ends up in brand set limbo, that netherworld where the brand is an acceptable choice for everyone, but not the preferred choice for anyone. Many very good brand portfolios such as Montgomery Ward, Oldsmobile, and Howard Johnson have fallen into that hole.

The alternative is what's called scaling: allowing the brand portfolio to follow its natural market, and then creating another portfolio to fill the upmarket or downmarket void. (Sometimes the portfolio that fills the void is new, but it can also be built off the original portfolio. In this case, scaling works as long as the tangential brand is well and wholly separated from the portfolio that has moved.)

We'll talk first about the upscaling alternative—the easier of the two to accomplish. Upscaling is a two-part strategy. First, a brand portfolio is either repositioned upmarket or allowed to evolve upmarket, following its customer base. The brand portfolio thus becomes a more upscale offering, which serves a more upscale demographic. Stage two is to replace the upscaled brand with another portfolio. The new brand backfills the vacated space.

Consider Gap. It is a great example of a portfolio that has sucessfully completed an upscaling strategy. Its revenues have skyrocketed from under $6 billion in 1996 to over $11.5 billion at the end of 1999. From the get go, Gap catered to teens. (The name was an abbreviation for "the generation gap.") But as its customer base grew older, Gap evolved to meet more sophisticated tastes, updated its brand and its value proposition, and extended its offerings: GapKids, BabyGap, GapBody. All these extensions catered to a baby boomer target.

To stay in touch with teens, Gap created a new brand, Old Navy, which has become today's leading fashion outlet for teens. Gap has successfully upscaled its brand portfolio and systematically backfilled with the Old Navy, thus holding onto the precious teen group.[3]

Downscaling is much harder. We'll go into more detail about that shortly. The brand portfolio manager must make a conscious decision not to let the portfolio migrate upward or at least to slow its migration. Usually this means installing an upscale brand portfolio to block your own growth. That's a very hard idea for most of us to get our heads around.

Both Honda and Toyota, for example, successfully kept the base portfolio downmarket and created upmarket brand portfolios, Acura and Lexus, respectively. (It's a safe bet some in Tokyo argued against the new portfolio, instead making a pitch to put the new high-end models under the Toyota brand portfolio.) Doing so allowed them to participate in the upscale markets but keep the Honda and Toyota portfolios reasonably focused on lower-price-point markets, with excellent results. In 2000, Toyota and Honda each had two of the ten top-selling cars in America. Toyota's Camry was number one, and the Corolla was seventh. Honda's Accord came in second and the Civic fourth.

Let's take a closer look at why upscaling and backfilling is easier than downscaling. First, enhancing product offerings is a natural phenomenon.[4] R&D continually turns out new improvements, and as brand equity grows over time, it's easier to support price increases. Even though Honda has not followed the market up into luxury cars, its base portfolio has edged upward. The once tiny Honda Civic is now a family sedan. In 1994, the Accord added two cylinders, seven centimeters in car length, and bigger tires to become a V-6 midsize.[5] In the process, the manufacturer's suggested retail price (MSRP) went from $19,930 to $22,030. Successful brand portfolios naturally float upward. Equally important, typically organizations have the skills and resources they need to backfill the hole in the market they leave behind. These include both internal resources, such as manufacturing capabilities, and external resources, such as distribution channel relationships.

In many instances, a company that has been successful in upscaling its brand has an advantage in backfilling. At least it should. First, the company likely has spent much of its past efforts understanding and serving, albeit less and less, the incumbent customer market. That experience and fact base should translate into advantage in reentering the space. Second, a very clear and tight value proposition for a successful upscaled brand should aid in the development of a tight value proposition and positioning for the backfilled brand. They should be mutually exclusive and complementary, with little or no overlap in customer demographic. Having a strong upscaled brand can only help in defining what is missing in the portfolio. It is typically much harder to create a new upmarket portfolio if the company has never competed in that market.

Not that either is easy. We spoke earlier of the challenges of positioning and repositioning. A true upscaling or downscaling strategy requires both simultaneously.

The Devil or the Deep Blue Sea?

Nonetheless, it is critical to try. Just as spanning the spreading segments is not an option, neither is just moving up or down and leaving a hole for competitors to enter. In 1949, the Haloid Company commercialized xerography with the Model A copier. In 1955, it took the business world by storm with its Xerox

Copyflo. By 1974, Xerox, formerly Haloid, was so dominant in its office copier products that the Federal Trade Commission (FTC) required the company to license its technologies.[6]

In the 1980s, Xerox branched outward and upward, purchasing companies specializing in optical character recognition, scanning, faxing, and desktop publishing. All were emerging, higher-priced technologies at the time. Soon to follow was entry into computer printing engines and networked color printers. The Xerox brand was continually upscaled, serving more technically savvy businesses with more technically oriented products. With its focus on the upscaled offering, Xerox never did backfill with a brand portfolio to serve the lower-priced copier franchise. Meanwhile digital copiers moved into the market, eroding Xerox's base. This not only cost Xerox volume, but also created a platform from which Canon and Ricoh could launch their own upscale products to attack Xerox's core market. Leaving a hole in the market has cost Xerox in copiers, IBM in data storage, and Kodak in cameras. Better to backfill with a new portfolio.

It is just as wise to create new portfolios to fill emerging spaces upstream. Rolex started its heralded franchise in 1908 in London and built one of the world's premiere luxury brands in the decades to follow.[7] But despite its high quality and price, Rolex sells over 600,000 watches worldwide.[8] Today, Rolex is considered in some circles to be a mass-market watch. It's no big deal to have an Oyster Perpetual on your wrist in the year 2000.

But Rolex saw this coming. At the time Rolexes were becoming mainstream, in the 1970s, the company formed its Cellini line, in tribute, as Rolex promotes, to Benvenuto Cellini, sculptor and goldsmith to renaissance kings and popes. This line offers densely jeweled timepieces that today have price tags that can exceed $1 million, many in the range of $500,000. Demand for the Cellini line has increased in each of the past seven years.[9] With Cellini, Rolex more than successfully "up-filled." It ensured that the company would continue to own the high ground of luxury timepieces without overstretching the core brand portfolio.

Summary

Scaling is a two-part strategy that can drive real growth for a brand portfolio. First, a core brand is, formally or informally, moved either upstream or downstream for customer markets; then a new brand portfolio is created in the vacated space. This act of backfilling the initial position of the core brand can be done with either a new brand or with a brand already in the portfolio. Most often, the repositioning or upscaling of a brand takes place first. The existence of a new customer base for the moved brand is the key to successful scaling. The upscaled or downscaled brand should be distinct but complementary to its brethren.

Keys to Success

1. Create tight and discrete positionings for the upscaled and downscaled brands, distinct from the existing portfolio. Old Navy is not Gap Lite. It is its own brand portfolio, with its own range, look, and feel. Nor is Banana Republic Gap Deluxe.

2. Allow the new portfolio to succeed. In 1997, when Absolut wanted to counter the emergence of higher-end competitors, it created a new upscale portfolio, Sundsvail. But Absolut continued to agonize over the potential cannibalization of Absolut by the new brand and dithered over Sundsvail strategy and rollout.[10] Allowing it to succeed means separating out the operations and leadership of the new portfolio from day zero. Saturn became the most successful new car portfolio launch in history at least in part because it was in California, far from Detroit.[11]

3. Be preemptive. Begin developing the new portfolio well before the segmenting market requires it. Levi watched designer jeans make inroads for years and did not react. Now it may be too late.

15

using the tools

Give us the tools, and we will finish the job.
—Winston Churchill, *February 9, 1941*

WE HAVE PROVIDED EIGHT TOOLS to manage the brand portfolio. Is this the complete toolkit? Perhaps not. Snap-On is one of the leading suppliers of tools to mechanics. Every year, it adds new tools because as engines change so do the tools required to work on them. We expect the brand portfolio manager's toolkit will grow as well.

If you're reading this book, it's a good bet you've used some of these tools before on your brands. That may be, but using them on your portfolio is going to pose a new challenge. For one thing, you'll find yourself bumping into more parts of your own organization and sitting down with managers from other companies. The moves you want to make will be bigger and more complicated, meaning they'll take longer and need to be more carefully laid out. Less day trading, more investing. Instead of discrete, stand-alone tactical activities, you'll be creating strategic programs that combine several tools and plans to meet a single objective.

You'll need to create a new discipline in the organization, convincing more people that fewer right moves are better than more not-so-right ones. You and your colleagues will need to consider the possibility that every brand extension, once created, will live forever; that an alliance to another portfolio is marriage without divorce; that for every brand portfolio there is a small and finite number of strategic moves, and that each move must be used wisely. (None of these assumptions is strictly true. But working as if they were encourages thoughtfulness and strategic thinking.)

You'll need to make sure the right measures are in place. This month's share report isn't going to tell the whole story. Occasionally, a new brand or portfolio will achieve rapid, widespread awareness, such as Amazon.com did. But more likely you will need time to implement the portfolio approach and then see the payoff in loyalty or price premiums.[1] "New" brands such as Microsoft, Cisco, and EMC are twenty-five, fourteen, and twenty-one years old, respectively. Some initiatives, like co-branding or partitioning, will pay off immediately. Others—extension, pruning, repositioning, and so on—will take time to roll out and see the results.

The results will be there. Good portfolio management will roll up the value between brands and create new value in the empty spaces where no value had previously existed. It will accelerate growth and reduce risk. It will be a whole new way to create brand value.

Let's look at three cases of how these tools might be used to create this value: Cadillac, PING, and Miller Beer. We've worked for one of these three before, although we've been careful to build this case from publicly available data. We will talk through each case exactly as we would were we advising those managers.

Cadillac

In chapter 3, we discussed the incredible challenge facing Cadillac marketers. They must restore the brand's relevance to a new generation of luxury car buyers, forty-somethings now buying full-sized vehicles like Mercedes, Volvos, and sports utility vehicles (SUVs) of all kinds, but who wouldn't be caught dead with a Caddie in the driveway. Doing this is going to require some serious portfolio surgery.

Before we can get to our main objective, we first need to do a little basic maintenance. The first thing we notice about the BPM shown in figure 15-1 is that it is very cluttered. If we could, we'd cut out the ghost brands like Allante and Cimarron, but unfortunately, we have no tool to reach inside consumers' minds and erase neurons. But we can cut out many of the smaller support brands, such as Zebrano wood, PASS-Key II, Twilight Sentinel, and Magnasteer.

Let's also prune OnStar and Night Vision. We can keep the technologies but drop the brands. Since both are now available to other GM car divisions and to other car companies, they no longer provide a unique point of difference and we can do without them, despite their positives. And by cutting out these peripheral brands, we also manage to push Toyota and Saab, soon to carry OnStar aboard some of their own cars, back from the boundaries of our portfolio. This pruning has not only made the portfolio more manageable, but it has also freed up resources used to support OnStar and Night Vision, resources we can use to push our brand portfolio. Finally, before we are done pruning, let's get rid of the Senior PGA Tour affiliation. It cannot possibly further the objective of moving the portfolio toward a younger audience.

Now, let's try to work toward the main objective, making the portfolio more attractive to a younger audience. It's going to take repositioning. Of course, as we pointed out earlier, rejuvenating the core is always an alternative to repositioning. That is, rather than tacitly apologizing for the full-bodied, soft-as-a-sofa ride of cars such as DeVille, we could celebrate it, put some kind of retro-cool spin on it. (We think that's a pretty good option actually, but we know from observation that it is at odds with where GM wants to take the portfolio.) So let's scratch it off the list and work instead on repositioning the portfolio.

But we don't think DeVille and Eldorado can be repositioned, at least not where we want them. What if we partitioned

FIGURE 15-1

Brand Portfolio Molecule: Cadillac, 2000

Steinmetz-Opel

Catera
DHS
DTS

DeVille

Caddie
Seville
STS
Evoq
Le Mans Racing
SLS

Escalade

Team Cadillac

Pebble Beach
Senior PGA Tour
EWGA

PGA

Allante
Elvis Presley

Fleetwood
Cimarron
Potamkin (etc.)

Eldorado

Bose
Michelin
Cadillac
Bosch
Magnasteer
StabiliTrak
OnStar
Toyota
Northstar

Twilight Sentinel

Night Vision
Zebrano wood
General Motors
PASS-Key II

off the DeVille and Eldorado brands, or even amalgamated them with another division? That would allow us to retire the Seville, Escalade, and Catera brands and in their place insert a set of alphanumeric model numbers. The move would make the portfolio simpler to manage. What's more, the current generation of our target car buyers is more familiar with luxury car models rendered in letters and numbers, à la Mercedes SL. So to begin the repositioning process, let's first change the names.

Now let's go another step. Let's create a set of interstitial extensions around performance. First, let's rush the Evoq sports car, if not its model name, into the mix. Second, let's take the Steinmetz-Opel Catera idea and expand it across the entire range. For every Cadillac, let's offer the consumer a serious performance option.

Next, we can amplify these changes by creating a new set of alliances and co-brands, not only with the Le Mans Racing Series, but with Formula 1 or CART, as well as other sports links, such as to golf's feeder tours, soccer, or minor league baseball. We have other options, of course. We might consider sponsorship of a major rock and roll tour. If we really want to send a new signal, how about Britney Spears or Eminem? (Just kidding there.) Figure 15-2 shows the new portfolio. What do you think?

We think the new portfolio would move Cadillac very far toward meeting its strategic challenge. Everything we've suggested is doable. But we could not have recommended these changes when we worked for Cadillac in 1998. Why not? We didn't have the tools to think about the portfolio from this new 360-degree perspective. Now we do. By using pruning, repositioning, partitioning, amalgamation, extension, and co-branding, we can fundamentally restructure this portfolio to deliver against the strategic objectives. Let's try the process and the toolkit on two portfolios we have never worked on.

PING

The first time Karsten Solheim picked up a golf club, he was a forty-two-year-old engineer working for GE in Ithaca, New York. He became keenly interested in golf as a hobby, and after three years of frustration on putting greens, he developed the first heel

FIGURE 15-2

A Hypothetical Molecular View of the Cadillac Brand

Catera
DeVille

A Series

C Series

D Series
Steinmetz-Opel

Evoq

Le Mans Racing

LIGT

Escalade
NAG
AGA
Team Cadillac
Buy.com Tour
Pebble Beach
PGA

EWGA

PGA Europe

Eldorado
Allante

Cimarron
Fleetwood

Potamkin (etc.)

Bose

Michelin
Cadillac
Bosch

StabiliTrak

Northstar

General Motors

Figure 15-2 is a hypothetical BPM for Cadillac. It is our suggestion of how the Cadillac BPM in figure 15-1 should be reconfigured in order to meet the strategic challenge of bringing younger drivers into the franchise.

and toe balanced putter, a design that is the basis for almost all golf clubs today. In 1959, he began selling the PING putter. Since that time, Karsten had poured out an almost constant stream of innovations: investment casting and perimeter weighting for irons, heel and toe weighting for any type of club, the Cushin insert inside shafts, stand-up carry bags, and custom fitting.

In some ways, the Karsten brand molecule is wonderfully clean. It is just about golf. Major brands PING, EYE, ZING, ISI, and i3 are all types of clubs. There have been numerous branded add-ons close to the core offerings: a suite of hosels (small pieces attaching blade to shaft), six types of Cushin shafts, seven related types of shafts, and a set of grips. It is a dense cluster of brands with very high levels of interconnectedness and control, as well as a core of several strong positive brands in the eyes of customers (e.g., EYE, ZING, and i3). There are very few external elements of the PING portfolio, shown in figure 15-3. NASCAR, Pal Junior and the Karsten Cup are the only three significant events that show up in the portfolio.[2]

The challenge for Karsten, in our judgment, is that other golf companies have jumped on the innovation bandwagon. Now PING must compete with the more promoted brand portfolios of Callaway, Taylor Made, and Titleist and their hot new technologies like Big Bertha, Hawk Eye, Burner Bubble, and ti.

First, as with Cadillac, let's do a little basic maintenance. With no offense whatsoever to Mr. Solheim, the current brand portfolio looks like it was built by an engineer.[3] We have no doubt that all the different names and ingredient brands mean something, but we're avid golfers, and one of us is an engineer, and even we can't decipher what all these brands mean. Instead of straight pruning, let's amalgamate clusters of piece-part brands. Cushin shafts, now JZ-A, JZ-R, Z25, Fushion, Z-Z65, all roll into the Cushin brand. Likewise, the related ladies shafts, K-101, K-201, K-301, W54, X65, U34, all roll into Cushin Ladies. We'll do the same for the set of individual hosel brands, but bring it closer to the core by over-branding it PING Hosel. We hypothesize that these efforts would clean up the clutter quite a bit without losing much volume, since most are add-ons to club purchases.

FIGURE 15-3

First-Cut Brand Portfolio Molecule: PING, 2000

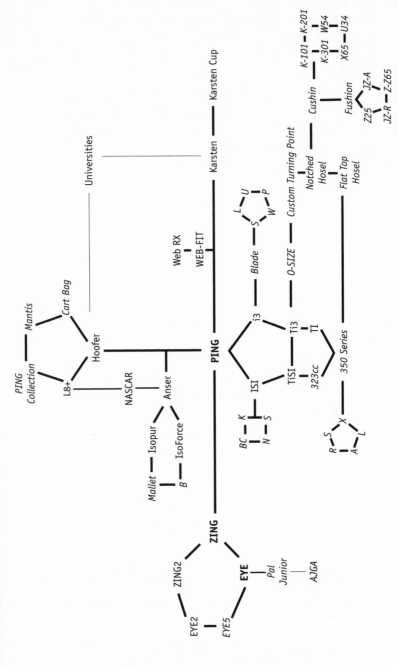

Figure 15-3 is a first-cut BPM for PING, a popular brand of golf clubs manufactured by Karsten. In total there are fifty-eight brands in the molecule.

Now let's rework the portfolio to compete better against the upstart rivals. Our BPM shows that the new lines offered by Karsten, specifically the Ti3, i3, TiSI, and ISI Tour, are in close proximity with each other, but far from the powerful incumbent brands of EYE and ZING. Let's partition that set of new brands, all the I lines, into a powerhouse mass brand to fight against Big Bertha. Included in that partition will be the Karsten brand, which will add credibility around the technology facets of the line. That line will receive most of the company's promotional dollars and will also benefit from a new set of external alliances with leading professional golfers, golf ball companies, and PGA events. It will also be sold in the more traditional sporting goods outlets. So now we have two distinct molecules: Karsten and PING.

PING, ZING, and EYE all are older, well-established brands, created in the early days of the franchise. Many golfers still use these clubs proudly. For them, PING, ZING, and EYE are the standards. These brands can withstand attacks by new technologies. Let's drive PING, ZING, and EYE together and push the customization angle. We will formally brand the customization that occurs with every purchase of each as The PING Fit. What about offering new services on the PING ZING line, to make it a customized hand-me-down club from parents to young golfers? My First PING services would fully refurbish every inch of the set. Now that we have pushed these brands together and revitalized them for a caring segment, we have the opportunity to up-fill against an attractive demographic.

PING began as the crème de la crème. Let's build on that. We would create an extension, The PING Standard, a line of irons that has the original PING deep edge but a sleeker more sophisticated line. We'd probably need to change the look to reinforce the new message, say titanium, gold, and brushed steel in combination throughout the blade. The grips are fine leather. Perhaps we'd put in a gold-plated putter as part of the collection. Each purchase happens only at a set of exclusive country clubs throughout the world, like Augusta, Winged Foot, Pebble Beach, and Congressional. Each club is custom fitted, with hand molds created for the grips. Every set is only sold after so-

FIGURE 15-4

Brand Portfolio Molecule: PING, Hypothetical

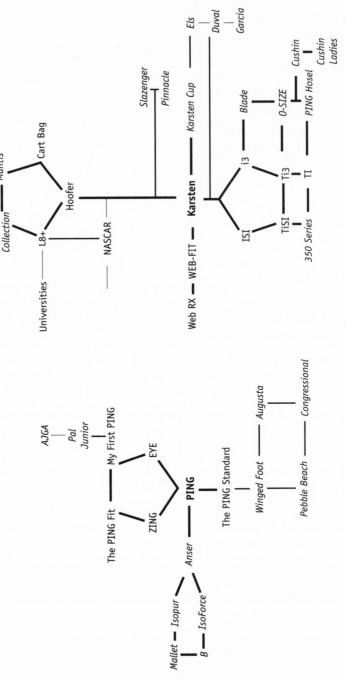

Figure 15-4 is a hypothetical BPM for PING. It is our suggestion of how the first-cut PING BPM in figure 15-3 should be reconfigured in order to meet the strategic challenge of increased competition within the category.

phisticated technical swing analyses. Each is hand-signed by the maker. Instead of catering to a golf market, where the newest thing rules, the PING molecule, shown in figure 15-4, would make the argument that a fine set of clubs is a once-in-a-lifetime luxury, tapping the timeless aspect of the sport.

Is this the right strategy for PING? Perhaps. More likely it is one of dozens that a brand portfolio manager could create with the toolkit. Only analysis and shrewd judgment will tell us which is best. That's OK. We bet Mr. Solheim did not come up with just one new design and start making it. We suspect there's a whole barrel of club designs that never made it. He probably designed them and then tested each, finding out which were best. The same logic applies to brand molecule designs.

Miller Beer

In chapter 5, we talked about the forces that shape brand portfolios. Time created the Cadillac molecule. The Karsten portfolio looks the way it does because of management approach. It was created with a focus on innovation and technology, with branding more as an afterthought. Miller Beer is also a portfolio created by management approach, but in this case a hyperactive focus on brand at the expense of the overall portfolio.

Miller Brewing Company had only a small handful of brands in 1972, when Philip Morris acquired it. Since that time, Miller has grown to a collection of molecules with over eighty-two trade names (listed in table 15-1), not including its various sponsorship and promotional sub-brand assets, such as MGD Music Productions, that create dozens of interconnections with other external portfolios. The Miller Beer molecule itself, shown in figure 15-5, is relatively small.

The Miller brand portfolio faces many challenges. It is disadvantaged in size versus the much larger Budweiser molecule, a tangible disadvantage in an advertising-intensive category. Recent advertising has been poor, so poor that it hurt sales. Most important though, is a deteriorating brand portfolio. Earlier we spoke of the importance of the brands in a portfolio having different roles. In Miller's portfolio all the brands are

TABLE 15-1

Miller Brands, 2000

Miller Trademark Brands	Brands Acquired in 2000	Plank Road Brewery Brands	Jacob Leinenkugel Brewing Company Brands	Celis Brewery Brands	Shipyard Brewing Company Brands	Import Brands
Miller Lite	Henry Weinhard's Private Reserve	Red Dog	Leinenkugel's Original Premium	Celis White Export Ale	Shipyard Golden	Molson
Miller Lite Ice	Henry Weinhard's Dark	ICEHOUSE	Leinenkugel's Light	Celis Grand Cru	Goat Island Light Ale	Molson Export Ale
Miller Genuine Draft	Henry Weinhard's Porter	Southpaw Light	Leinenkugel's Northwoods Lager	Celis Pale Ale	Fuggles Pale Ale	Molson Canadian
Miller Genuine Draft Lite	Henry Weinhard's Amber Ale	ICEHOUSE Light	Leinenkugel's Genuine Bock (seasonal)	Celis Golden	Old Thumper Extra Special Ale	Molson Canadian Light
Miller High Life	Henry Weinhard's Pale Ale		Leinenkugel's Red Lager	Celis Raspberry	Blue Fin Stout	Molson Light
Miller High Life Light	Henry Weinhard's Hazelnut Stout		Leinenkugel's Winter Lager (seasonal)	Celis Dubbel Ale	Longfellow Winter Ale (seasonal)	Molson Ice
Miller High Life Ice	Henry Weinhard's Blackberry Wheat		Leinenkugel's Autumn Gold	Pale Rider Ale	Longfellow India Pale Ale	Molson Exel non-alcohol

Miller Beer

Henry Weinhard's Hefeweizen

Henry Weinhard's Red Lager

Sharp's non-alcohol brew

Hamm's

Milwaukee's Best

Milwaukee's Best Light

Hamm's Draft

Milwaukee's Best Ice

Hamm's Special Light

Meister Bräu

Olde English 800 Malt Liquor

Meister Bräu Light

Olde English 800 Ice

Magnum Malt Liquor

Mickey's Malt Liquor

Mickey's Ice

(seasonal)

Leinenkugel's Honey Weiss

Leinenkugel's Berry Weiss (seasonal)

Leinenkugel's Auburn Ale

Leinenkugel's Big Butt Doppelbock (seasonal)

Leinenkugel's Maple Brown Lager

Leinenkugel's Creamy Draft (draft only)

Leinenkugel's Hefeweizen (draft only)

(seasonal)

Mystic Seaport Pale Ale

Chamberlain Pale Ale

Sirius Summer Wheat Ale (seasonal)

Prelude Ale (seasonal)

brew

Molson Red Jack Ale

Foster's Lager

Foster's Special Bitter

Sheaf Stout

*Presidente

**Shanghai

*from Cervecería Nacional Dominicana, Santa Domingo, Dominican Republic
**from Shanghai Foster's Brewery Co. Ltd., Shanghai, People's Republic of China

FIGURE 15-5

First-Cut Brand Portfolio Molecule: Miller, 2000

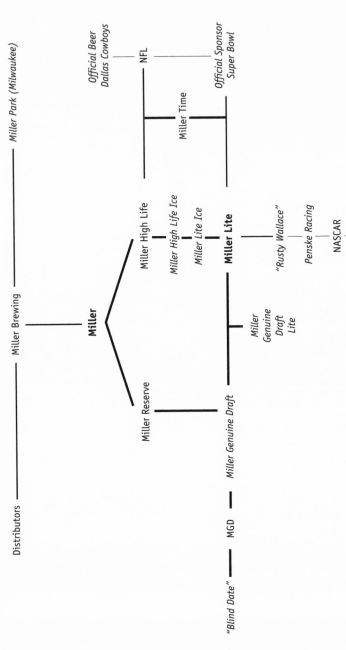

Figure 15-5 is a first-cut BPM for Miller beer. In total there are twenty brands in the molecule.

attacking the same markets and have mixed-and-matched brand equities to the extent that the Miller portfolio looks less like a molecule than an amorphous clump. Let's look at how the portfolio got here.

In the mid-1990s, Miller was caught between two powerful forces: profit-ravaging price wars with Anheuseur-Busch and encroachment by microbrewers. Lite remained the top seller in the Miller portfolio. High Life was declining and increasingly competing in the price category. Miller Genuine Draft had done well in some markets but faltered in too many to continue to spend heavily to advertise it nationally. Red Dog was doing well, but it had been introduced craftily under the aegis of the Plank Road Brewery, making it thoroughly disconnected from the Miller name.[4]

In 1995, Miller CEO Jack McDonough recognized that the Miller portfolio lacked a strong lead brand and as a result was floundering. He initiated a project called "Spinnaker," intended to establish the kind of brand asset McDonough had enjoyed in his days as an Anheuseur-Busch executive: a premium, full-calorie flagship brand. He decided to launch Miller Beer.

It was not successful. Miller found confusion among consumers as to what all the hullabaloo was about, since they'd already heard of Miller beers in various permutations. Miller Brewing Company rolled out a flight of ads specifically to distinguish Miller Beer from other Miller products such as High Life and Genuine Draft.[5] Consumers didn't buy it, in either sense. McDonough hoped to tie up all of Miller's brands with one golden standard, whose halo would grace the rest of Miller's portfolio. Further, Miller had even made a more earnest attempt to create a true premium entry with an earlier, well-reviewed but ill-received brand called Miller Reserve. In September of the same year, Gerry Khermouch reported that Miller was redirecting Miller Beer support funds back into Lite.[6]

In fact, the launch of Miller Beer not only did not help the portfolio, it had a negative effect by diverting resources from other brands in the portfolio and in other brand portfolios. After spending around $40 million in media on Genuine Draft and $60 million on Red Dog in 1995, Miller liberally raided those war chests, including the siphoning of most of Red Dog's budget, to fund the national Miller Beer launch, starting in February 1996.[7] Even High Life found dollars of its by-then-meager budget diverted to the effort. Miller went through four ad agencies and three different campaigns. In October, the company undertook a downsizing and restructuring of its marketing department. Miller then returned to its Lite brand as its lead trademark.

Today, Miller continues to go through management changes and brand repositionings. Much of the promotional efforts being conducted continue to push the brands together, creating a lack of uniqueness and differentiation across the portfolio. In 1999, Miller promoted Miller Genuine Draft, MGD. Miller Genuine Draft Light, and Miller Lite together, letting consumers develop custom CDs on the CDNOW Web site once they found a lucky bottle top.[8] Late in 2000, Miller used several of its brands in Hispanic efforts: Miller Lite sponsored Texas's Title Belt Hispanic Boxing Events, Miller Genuine Draft sponsored the Mexican National Soccer team, and MGD sponsored the Solo Con Invitacion music program.[9] The brands continued to be seen as interchangeable, from both inside and outside.

The Miller brand portfolio needs to create fewer, more differentiated brands—that is, simplify it and open it up. And it needs to build a true strong lead brand, rather than letting the different brands take turns. Finally, all these strategies need some time to take hold.

From a consumer perspective, both Miller Beer and Miller High Life are one and the same, so let's amalgamate those two brands into Miller High Life. Then, since Miller Genuine Draft and MGD are so close, let's promote MGD over Miller Genuine Draft and lose the longer brand name. That shortening will inevitably drive some needed distance between Miller High Life and MGD.

Then let's work on the positionings of those two big brands. For Miller High Life, let's put our money where the name is. Let's get some partners for the brand that bring it to its core: the Jazz Age, and a sophisticated time past. Harry Connick Jr. or Wynton Marsalis as spokesman. Substantial affiliations with the Newport Jazz Festival or leading cutting-edge jazz events at Lincoln Center. An annual contribution to Juilliard would be a nice touch. Also, let's put a small Miller High Life refrigerator

FIGURE 15-6

Brand Portfolio Molecule: Miller, Hypothetical

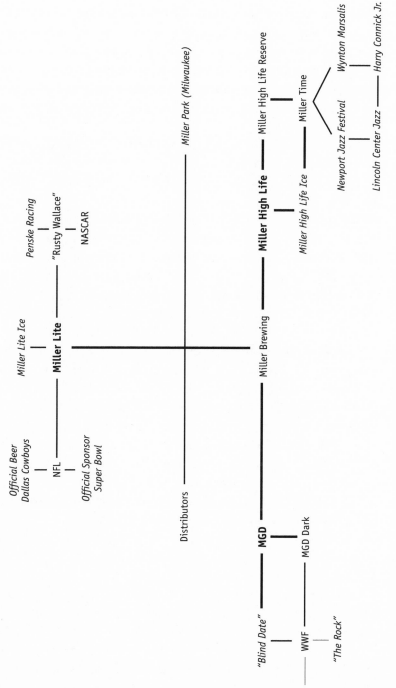

Figure 15-6 is a hypothetical BPM for Miller. It is our suggestion of how the Miller BPM in figure 15-5 should be reconfigured in order to meet the strategic challenge of customer confusion, and lack of loyalty to the Miller High Life brand.

in all the cigar stores in the major metro markets to tie into the nostalgia. Stay the course here for some time.

For MGD, let's go young and hard to create space between the brands. Partnerships could focus on gen Xers. We could partner MGD with the X-Games and the top-rated sports challenge programs. Let a professional wrestler, say The Rock, promote MGD on air and in ring. Last, stay the course with Miller Lite and lead with Lite, not Miller. That brand lives in a strong separate space from both Miller High Life and MGD and should stay there. (See figure 15-6)

Again, as with Cadillac and PING, the plan we've outlined for Miller is an option, not the *one right answer*. But whatever Miller managers do, they should do it for more than a quarter. Although Budweiser has used over thirty advertising tag lines in the last century, it has been careful to maintain the same overall positioning throughout, usually through use of multiple tag lines and two different ad campaigns running simultaneously. After launching Budweiser at the end of the nineteenth century as the "King of Bottled Beers," Anheuser-Busch has publicly buttressed its status as "King of All Bottled Beers" (1906–1950, except during Prohibition) or the "King of Beers" ever since. Every element of the brand system has supported that claim, from packaging to quality claims to line extensions. This rigidly singular focus even led the company to agonize for seven long years after the 1975 launch of Miller Lite before finally committing to Bud Light. Anheuser-Busch executives feared a light beer would fail to deliver against the brand system promise. Miller would profit from a similar, more strategic approach to portfolio management.

Summary

We spoke earlier of brand portfolios being overadministered and undermanaged. Hopefully, by explaining the tools in some depth, the distinction we are making is now a bit clearer. We also spoke of the tools being different from those used with brands. Positioning is usually thought of as a quick fix to boost the brand by creating a new tag line for the advertising. We speak of repo-

sitioning the portfolio as a time-consuming exercise that may require a whole host of strategic moves to deliver the new promise.

This is a big idea, and one with far-reaching organizational
implications. In Part 3 we look at what the implications are
and at two organizations that have begun grappling with them
successfully.

implementing brand
portfolio
management

16

brand portfolio management— the 3M case

There is nothing to it. You only have to hit the right note at the right time and the instrument plays itself.
—Johann Sebastian Bach

MOVING TO a brand portfolio approach—rethinking the fundamentals of using brands to increase returns and manage risk and optimizing the portfolio using the toolkit—requires a new type of organization. First, it creates the need for a new role, the brand portfolio manager, who can see across business units and individual brands. Ford not long ago formed a company within a company called the Premier Auto Group (PAG). Intended to optimize a subset of acquired and traditional brands, PAG groups the Jaguar, Volvo, Aston Martin, Lincoln, and Land Rover brand portfolios under a single manager charged with creating a luxury car entity to rival Mercedes within a few years.[1] The brand portfolio manager is a very critical role. It is this manager who sets portfolio vision and guidelines, resolves conflicts between brand managers over uses of the brand, and decides when and where to use the toolkit.

In addition, moving to a portfolio approach requires changing the culture of the organization. Brand managers must balance championing their individual brands with thinking through the long-term best interests of the portfolio. They must begin thinking of brands as assets and of measuring risk and return. Indeed, in the brand-portfolio-based organization, everyone must begin thinking of the brand portfolio as assets— to be maintained, conserved, and built.

We have not found any organization that is all the way there. One that is very far along, however, is 3M™. The company's history is that of a technology-driven manufacturing company and, like most industrial companies, 3M started with a distinct nonchalance toward branding and skepticism toward marketing. But in spite of the skepticism, or perhaps because of it, 3M has really pushed the concept of brand portfolio management forward. The company has created a role similar to our brand portfolio manager, has begun delineating brand portfolios and creating visions and guidelines for each, and has begun defining ways to measure return.[2]

Background

A Fortune 100 company and one of the foundation companies that make up the Dow Jones Industrial Index, 3M chalked up nearly $16 billion in revenues in 1999 and employed over 70,000 people around the world.[3]

The company began in 1902 as a producer and seller, first of coated abrasives and then tapes, such as masking tape and its first famous branded product, Scotch® Transparent Tape. From there, the research and technology engine at 3M generated a bevy of related products and whole product categories:

- pressure-sensitive tapes for applications ranging from consumer and office to heavy industrial uses,

- roofing granules for shingles,

- reflective sheeting for traffic signs, license plates, and vehicle markings,

- surgical tapes for the medical profession, and, more recently,

- fiber-optic connectors, microelectronic circuitry, and other e-commerce backbone materials that stem from core technologies in light management, coatings, films, and pressure-sensitive adhesives.

Today, the 3M organization consists of more than forty product divisions grouped into six global business segments ("market centers"), as well as several corporate staff groups and an international group that coordinates the work of over sixty 3M subsidiaries around the world. While three of these segments—Industrial Markets; Transportation, Graphics and Safety Markets; and Health Care Markets—account for more than 60 percent of 3M revenues, they rely on a relatively smaller number of brands. On the other hand, Consumer and Office Markets, which accounted for about 17 percent of the company's revenues in 2000, holds the majority of 3M's most widely known brands. (See table 16-1.)

The 3M brand portfolio is interesting for several reasons. The first is that, despite its relatively recent focus on brands, 3M has created some very strong brands, like Scotch and Post-it®. In addition, 3M has created a lot of brands. Most of these are smaller brands, many related to specific technologies. The company still calls its smaller brands "trademarks."

Also interesting is that unlike classic brand management organizations where one manager "owns" a brand and controls all marketing communication for that brand, at 3M, brands are often shared across multiple business units. Seven different business units share the Scotch brand. In the mid-1990s, 3M began a concerted effort to better understand and manage this complex and difficult brand portfolio.

From Trademarks to Brands

Dean Adams, director of corporate brand management, leads the 3M Corporate Brand Department. This group is the closest we have found to a true "brand portfolio manager." A few knickknacks adorn Adams's office, among them a time-worn, homemade poster showing the family of 3M brands. On closer look, numerous elements of the portrait appear out of whack, at least from the standpoint of today's brand portfolio. There are familiar brands with unfamiliar logos. There are unfamiliar brands placed prominently next to brands that are household names. And there is a disturbing complexity to the grouping of

TABLE 16-1

Summary of 3M Business Divisions

Division	% 2000 Revenues	Visible Brands
Industrial Markets	21%	Scotch Scotchgard™ 3M Perfect-It™ Trizact™ Scotch-Brite™
Transportation, Graphics and Safety Markets	21%	3M Scotchlite™ Scotchprint®
Health Care Markets	19%	Aldara™ Littmann®
Consumer and Office Markets	17%	Scotch Scotchgard Scotch-Brite Post-it O-Cel-O™ Nomad™
Electronic and Communications	15%	3M Microflex Volition™ Scotch
Specialty Materials	7%	3M Dyneon™ Scotchgard Novec™

Table 16-1 summarizes 3M's Operating Divisions. Total revenue for the corporation in 2000 was $19,659 million. A sample of brands—both leading and emerging—are listed in the right-hand column.

Source: Dow Jones Interactive (DJI), http://www.djinteractive.com. We reviewed the detailed company financials listed in the 3M company profile in DJI in order to compile the information listed in table 16-1.

3M brands circa 1993. The poster is there, Adams says, as a historical perspective, to "remind me of where 3M started."

Adams is by background a physicist, but has spent much of his 3M career in marketing. In 1993, he took a corporate marketing job "for a couple of years at best," or so he thought. His title was, in true 3M fashion of the time, Trademark Manager. At the time, brand management at 3M meant advertising management and execution. The Trademark Manager position sat within the Corporate Marketing group and was charged with acting as "logo-cop."

Adams's role required considerable interaction with the legal department, and it was there that he struck up an association with Bob Hoke, a trademark attorney with a long list of credentials. At the time, there was considerable discussion both outside and inside 3M over brands and how best to use them. Adams and Hoke began a dialogue on the subject. Over the next six months Adams voraciously scoured the popular press, "read a stack of books five feet high," as he recalled, and interviewed some of the best brand thinkers of the time.[4]

One voice that stood out in the din was that of consultant Larry Light. Adams and his fledgling team worked with Light to create a training program on brands that they hoped would "electrify the organization." They brought to their corps a message simple to grasp but essentially new thinking for the 3M organization. A trademark, they put forth, was not equal to a brand. Instead, *the brand is a promise that lives in the mind of the customer.*

This customer-centric redefinition was a significant shift for most of 3M. It raised the idea that there was more to a brand than a legal registration and a logo. There were the overall image and the users' experience, of course, but also connected brands. Adams even talked about the shape of a Scotch tape dispenser as part of the brand.

3M was intrigued, but it is a quantitatively driven company. The idea of brand was interesting, but how did it relate to the bottom line? The connection became clearer in 1995. The brand group had begun studying brand valuation methodologies in 1994, but had not yet begun collecting data. Then, while working on an advertising and distribution program with divisions that sold Post-it products, they had the opportunity to gather the data they needed. Their analysis established the value of the Post-it brand as not the millions they had imagined—but over a billion dollars. They quietly began discussing the findings internally.

Then in 1996, a reporter from *Financial World* called to discuss 3M's participation in its regular "Brand Value" issue. The magazine asked Adams to provide detailed volume and pricing data for the Scotch and Post-it brands. He refused, because the information requested is considered 3M proprietary.

Nine months later, *Financial World* called again. It had hired an outside consultant to value the 3M brands and simply wanted 3M's comment on the consultant's findings. *Financial World* had valued Post-it Notes at $1.1 billion, and the Scotch brand at $2.4 billion. Based on his earlier work, Adams said, "close enough." The information was published. The 3M brand valuation news went all the way up the chain in St. Paul. The phones started ringing down in Corporate Branding. "Who," senior management wanted to know, "is responsible for our brands? Are we managing brand assets with the same rigor with which we manage our patents and plants? How do we know if we are building or eroding brand assets?"

From Brand to Brand Portfolios

Even before the brand asset figures came in, though, 3M had begun to move beyond simply thinking of a brand as little more than a legal trademark. A key meeting in 1994 set the stage. Former CEO L. D. "Desi" DeSimone was a "prove-it-to-me" guy. Thus it was with some nervousness that Adams and his boss, Drew Davis, then vice president of corporate marketing and public affairs, first offered up a segmented pyramid for thinking about the 3M brand portfolio.

As you looked at the pyramid from bottom to top, each segment represented a smaller number of increasingly valuable brands—a subset of the 2,500 trademarks shown on the bottom row. The segment on the next row up represented 3M's more than 1,500 trademarks—all those registered. Of those registered trademarks, 300 were considered brands, distinguished from the segment below because each harbored some market value. Above that lay a shortlist of 100, deemed "powerful" brands. And the top triangle of the pyramid contained seven brands, each needing vital, active management because of the considerable value contained therein. These were Scotch, Post-it, Thinsulate,™ Scotchgard, Scotch-Brite, O-Cel-O, and 3M. It was the first brand molecule. The team need not have worried. DeSimone's response was, "Why only seven?" He gave the team his backing and lent his influence to spreading the brand message through top management ranks.

3M now wanted to push the concepts behind brand to a more practical level, where they could create new value. The first group to volunteer was the Post-it brand team from the Consumer and Office Division. Post-it products were a success story well before the team began grappling with the issues around brand. A constant stream of innovations had already put the product range into nearly every office in America.

First, 3M offered Post-it Notes in different colors, then preprinted ones for specific messages and purposes, then customized notes that allowed personal or company names to be preprinted in certain locations. Then came a set of nontraditional paper Post-it Notes: Pop-Up Notes, then little notes less than half the size of the original square pads. But even though still a relatively young brand, the Post-it brand was already becoming complex and difficult to manage.

Adams, Light, and the Post-it management team began a set of workshops to better understand the Post-it brands. At first, the team tried to coax a Post-it brand promise out of existing corporate opinion. The result did not wow anyone: "Post-it products contain a repositionable adhesive that meets a specific technical specification."[5]

The team commissioned a comprehensive research study to determine how end users conceived of the Post-it brand, conducting dozens and dozens of focus groups around the world, coupled with a complementary piece of quantitative research. It proved difficult from both a process and a content perspective. The data was complex because of the wide range of countries involved. Eventually the team was able to build a basis for a real, consumer-oriented brand snapshot. It was a difficult iterative process, but the results justified the effort. The new promise read: "Post-it products promise fast, friendly, repositionable communication and organization tools that help get the job done." This brand promise not only clarified the marketing charge and communications requirements, but also spread to the R&D departments in their development efforts and to the channel partners in their co-marketing work. The brand promise constituted the first step toward a brand portfolio vision and guidelines.

The study also led the Post-it team to restructure the portfolio. It made Post-it the lead brand of the portfolio, the clear central reason for purchase, around which all other brands in the portfolio revolved. A number of brands lingering in the portfolio became support brands, such as Snap-Ups and Premium Blue. It also prompted the company to take the Post-it brand off products that did not fit the brand promise, for example, glue sticks.

The biggest effect on this portfolio, however, was the addition of several new and significant brands. Without the old boundaries on the portfolio, the company created focused products with more direct connection to the lead brand and its newly defined promise: Post-it Software Notes (no paper, no adhesive), Post-it Easel Pads, Post-it Flags, and more. All these became significant brands for the line.[6] All had a clear growth-oriented position in the portfolio. The remapped Post-it portfolio also made a clear statement that the 3M brand is not the lead brand. In the company parlance, the 3M brand endorses the Post-it brand. The overall size of the Post-it portfolio remained relatively the same, but it grew tighter and more controllable.

The work on Post-it, of course, was only one element of the vision for the rest of the powerhouse brands atop the 3M pyramid. Even as Post-it underwent reconstruction, another twenty or so brand teams had begun to set up similar "laboratories."

Institutionalizing Brand Portfolio Management

Chuck Harstad, the vice president and general manager on Post-it Notes early on, later became the head of corporate marketing. Harstad provided clearance for much of the organizational barriers encountered along the way. It was Harstad, as much as anyone else, who turned brand portfolio management from an initiative into a way of doing business.

Early in 1998, Harstad was appointed to the helm of the Corporate Brand Management Committee, a group that, to that point, had been partially effective in spreading the process used by the Post-it brand team to other groups. Harstad agreed to chair the committee and immediately set about reconfiguring it. Step one was to redefine the objective, focusing it almost exclusively on building the asset value of the 3M brands. Then he enlisted CEO DeSimone as sponsor of the committee. He also changed the membership. The new committee included many of 3M's top officers, the senior vice president of marketing, the senior vice president of technology, two line executive vice presidents, the top trademark attorney, the area vice president for Europe, and the head of 3M public relations.

This team, with the steady support of Adams, Harstad, and consultant Light, continued working on strategy and policy for brand management at 3M. In February 1999, spearheaded by the European corporate marketing team, the committee developed a brand management policy that included a set of new brand designations as parameters for focus and strategy throughout 3M. The committee agreed on new brand designations of "authority brand," "strategic brand," and "product trademark" to drive all forthcoming efforts. (We found this simple three-tier structure so useful that we adopted it for our brand molecule mapping, although we found the terms "lead," "strategic," and "support" more useful to a broad audience.) They pushed this more granular and specific definition into the company.

The Brand Management Committee also established clear decision-making policies to help avoid and resolve brand portfolio conflicts. For example, this committee determined the criteria for designating a brand as one of 3M's strategic brands—a highly desirable designation, since it brings with it senior management and financial support, as well as internal prestige. To get this designation, a brand team must apply to the Brand Management Committee and receive its approval. The committee itself also helps resolve some of the tougher issues, such as deletions. More than anything, the organization now had a powerful advocate for brand portfolio management. And it also had a home to resolve issues not manageable at lower levels.

Beyond policy, Harstad pushed the team toward implementation. In January 2000, he orchestrated a multimillion-dollar research and tracking program to assess the progress in systematically moving all the lead brands at 3M. The plan calls for realignment along the elemental portfolio policy lines within three years, with budgets and processes accordingly redirected within line groups. He is also encouraging the systematic reassessment of each portfolio, and, as of this writing, the Scotch portfolio review is now under way, complete with massive research and deep manager involvement.

Concurrent with the work of the Brand Management Committee, 3M's Corporate Identity and eBusiness departments are developing a consistent brand approach for all of 3M's Web sites. 3M is making a hard audit of how 3M uses the Internet and the specific impact its e-commerce initiatives make on the overall brand portfolio. And it's bringing its new internal methodology to the process. For example, 3M executives have identified the implicit brand promise of *anything* the company does on the Internet: simplicity, ease of use, and speed.

Defining the brand promise of the dot-com brand is an important idea and agrees with our research. Once you take a brand into a new space, or combine it with something new, it becomes a brand of its own. That is, putting a ".com" behind a company name means that the brand promise, *overall*, must begin including those elements implicit in the Internet brand. This is clearly the brand portfolio mindset in action.

On the Horizon

It would be naïve to suggest that the transformation at 3M is complete. Managers still occasionally talk about narrow definition of a brand. And not everyone has bought into the idea of a more strategic (read: deliberate) approach to making portfolio decisions. But it is a very impressive start, even more so because of where it started. In our judgment, the work done at 3M can thus far serve as a good model of what might be done across many, many portfolios to make them run better. Few organizations can provide an example of such pervasive brand portfolio management in such a massive, far-reaching brand portfolio.

- Organization. 3M has created the role of brand portfolio manager and found ways to involve both senior and middle management in making brand portfolio decisions.

- Process. 3M has in place defined processes to set brand portfolio vision and guidelines.[7] It has a process for resolving disputes and for initiating "toolkit" actions to optimize the portfolio.

- Culture. By and large, everyone in 3M now understands brands as assets, and as assets with the potential for very high, even infinite, leverage.

3M is still working on aligning brand promise and "channel promise." Co-marketing alignments with partners can work, but their objectives should not muddle the ultimate purpose, which is to identify and profitably serve the best interests and desires of the end user. The company believes it needs to push even harder on data and measurement. Without hard qualitative and quantitative valuations, Adams insists, attempts to reframe a brand portfolio in accordance with the customer market become hollow, if not untenable.

Nonetheless, it is a useful case study. 3M is an industrial company, which shows not only that branding concepts are useful beyond narrow consumer package goods companies, but also that no one type of company has a monopoly on good thinking about brands. That the company moved from trademark management to brand portfolio management in only seven years speaks volumes about the robustness of the underlying concepts. And 3M's rigor in thinking through what it was trying to accomplish and its success at institutionalizing it provides a road map for other companies facing similar issues. In a word, if a company with the breadth and complexity of 3M can do it, you can do it.

17

overcoming organizational resistance

This time, like all times, is a very good one, if we but know what to do with it.
—Ralph Waldo Emerson, *"The American Scholar,"*
an oration delivered before the Phi Beta Kappa Society,
Cambridge, MA, August 31, 1837

WE THINK THE OPPORTUNITY for executives over the next decade will be to convert brand management organizations to brand portfolio management organizations. But nobody says it's going to be easy. Specifically, we see three barriers standing in the way:

- Differing definitions of the task at hand
- Short-term organizational priorities
- Increasing portfolio complexity

How well companies cope with these three issues will determine how quickly they're able to roll out brand portfolio management.

Transforming "Companies with Great Brands" into "Great Brand Portfolio Managers"

As we discussed in chapter 1, it seems that everyone has a different philosophical definition of brand. Don Sexton of Columbia University says he has collected seventeen, all different and all valid. What is more surprising is that everyone has a different *working* definition of brand or, more specifically, of *the brand*.

For example, when we speak to marketers at Porsche and they use the term *the brand*, they mean Porsche. For them Carrera and 911 are just product names. When we speak to some marketers at GM and they use the term *the brand*, they mean Corvette. For them, Chevrolet and GM are just division and corporate brands added for endorsement. Although there are clear differences between the two cars, at a basic level, Corvette and the 911 both offer competing value propositions to a similar market segment and are direct competitors. The two brands compete head-to-head. Yet the executives directing *the brands* are using fundamentally different definitions of the same word.

Every organization has its own view on what *the brand* is, based on its internal perspective. Here's another, less obvious example. At 3M, managers squirm when we insist that Post-it Notes and Post-it Self-Stick Table Top Pads are different strategic brands in a tight brand portfolio. They would say there is the Post-it brand. Period. But that's too simple.

Calling something a brand doesn't make it one. Not calling something a brand doesn't mean it isn't. Different names don't always mean different brands, and the same name doesn't mean the same brand. Consider some obvious examples. EMC, the data storage company, and EMC Insurance share the same name, but they're surely not the same brand. They're not even the same company. Nor are Helios Chemical Company, Helios Communications of New Zealand, Helios Software, Helios Consulting, and Helios Health.

Confusion usually occurs because the idea that consumers define *the brand* is a very difficult perspective to come to grips with. The argument that a single legal brand entity can be multiple consumer brands is an even harder idea to come to grips with. What makes it hard is that we automatically think about brands from the internal perspective. It's a bit like those Magic Eye drawings—"I can almost see it. No, there it goes again." We are repeating ourselves here, but if you want to realize the full potential, of brand portfolio management you have to force yourself to define brands and draw the lines between them based on the consumer's perspective. Is it hard to do? Yes. Are the lines blurry? Absolutely. But you have to keep at it. Assuming the problem will go away won't get you anywhere.

At the same time, we must also put aside parochial definitions of brand management. Brand management is about what you organize to do, not how you organize. Back to 3M and GM. At 3M, brand management means thinking of brands as assets and using corporate resources to coordinate the efforts of different divisions in defining the brand. But there is no single manager assigned to each brand, as there is at GM, where brand management means assigning each car line (e.g., Bonneville) to a manager who is responsible for developing it. There, just as at P&G, brand management is considered a line function, complete with a P&L. At 3M, brand management is carried out by staff. Both 3M and GM use the term "brand management" to describe their approaches. But they are talking about very different processes and organizational structures when they do so.

Is the definition really that important? We think so. Our former colleague Paul Branstad used to say, "The answer you come up with can depend on the handle you pick up the problem with." The working definitions of *the brand* and *brand management* have real implications for how receptive managers are to brand portfolio management. When executives automatically assume that optimizing their brand is their sole responsibility, it makes them reluctant to embrace brand portfolio management. And there is a real risk that opportunities will be missed because the right sort of strategic conversations aren't taking place.

In short, definition is a surprisingly complex topic. But it is not just semantics. A wrong definition can lead you to assume away the problem, and the opportunity, of brand portfolio management. To really tap the value of brands, we must move from "companies with great brands" to "great brand portfolio managers." The key, we think, is to force the exercise of defining the entire brand portfolio and doing so from the consumer's perspective.

Staying on Course through Changing Priorities

Only a few years ago, business experts sang requiems for the brand. "The 1990s are an era of brand consolidation. Brands will disappear," said Andrew Shore, an analyst with Prudential Securities in 1993.[1] Shore was not alone in his pessimism. Private labels, similarly formulated store-brand products without the slick packaging or marketing overhead, were growing impressively. The Food Marketing Institute estimated that retailers, and thus consumers, really didn't need 5 percent to 25 percent of the brands and sizes on their shelves. Mighty P&G had just eliminated White Cloud bathroom tissue, Top Job cleaner, and Puritan cooking oil.[2] A *Business Week* article was headed "Brands on the Run," playing off the title of an erstwhile Paul McCartney album.[3]

But rumors of the brand's demise turned out to be dead wrong. We have not seen a decrease in either the number or the importance of brands. "The Great Brand Despair of 1993" came and went, while brand discourse among a whole new generation of professionals, schooled in traditional corporate hallways but looking well beyond, has reached new heights. Just three years after all these dire predictions, a *Fortune* article titled "The Brand's the Thing" took a decidedly bullish stance on brands. "Brand seems to be on everybody's mind these days," the magazine posited in 1996. The enthusiasm has continued to build. A search for the word "brand" in 1993 in mass business periodicals revealed 78,598 hits. The same search in 1998 showed 220,642 hits.

The rise and fall of the brand in the media and among analysts mirrors—on a macro level—life inside the marketing department. An issue can go from the top of the agenda one day to the bottom another or vice versa.

Another day, another crisis, another budget cut to bring us down, another fresh new marketing idea to lift us up. Another buzzword is going to bump brand to the back of the bookshelf. It's the reality of marketing. But brand and brand portfolio management are too important just to be elbowed aside. You must find a way to really lock into the process of change. The answer we think lies in doing what Chuck Harstad at 3M did, creating the top-level buy into brands and driving the change downward. Don't let brand slide down the agenda.

Avoiding Being Overwhelmed by the Magnitude of the Problem

The final barrier to adoption lies in brand portfolios themselves. We are seeing an explosion in both the size and complexity of brand portfolios. As a result most marketing departments are frantically bailing out the boat. Creating the level of change we think is required will be difficult just because managers are too busy with day-to-day issues to make changes that would make it easier to deal with day-to-day issues. Brand portfolio management may be the answer, but can they afford to stop bailing long enough to fix the hull?

Just look at the number of brands in the market today. As we saw in chapter 16, using trademark as a definition of brand is a pretty primitive notion. Nonetheless, it is a very practical one if you want to count them. The United States Patent and Trademark Office tracks U.S. trademarks and servicemarks via a database called CASSIS, or the Classification and Search Support Information System.

To look at the growth in marks over time, we first tapped government sources to compile a universe of all marks, trademarks and servicemarks, for the four broad industry groups—motor vehicles, staple foods, distilled spirits, and finance and insurance. By universe, we mean all marks applied for, most of which are approved and a few of which are pending, since 1900. With this massive set in place, we combed through the set to eliminate duplication and make the data consistent. Specifically, we aligned differences in spelling and syntax (e.g., Ford and

Ford Motor were made into a standard Ford Motor Company), we eliminated duplicate trademarks and servicemarks, and we sorted the database by application date and then by industry group. This is where we began our analysis.

The results, shown in figure 17–1, exhibit proliferation of astounding proportions. Each of the four broad industries has seen a tremendous growth in the number of trademarks. On average, there are 3.6 times as many trademarks in these four categories than there were in 1990, and over twice as many as in 1993, when predictions of brand consolidation were so prevalent.

Even more interesting is to look at this growth over a recent time period, say the last decade, in comparison to the growth in revenues in the same four categories. For example, while revenues in motor vehicles have grown at a rate of 5.6 percent per year, the number of trademarks and servicemarks in those in-

FIGURE 17-1

Total New Brands Registered Selected Industries: 1984–1998

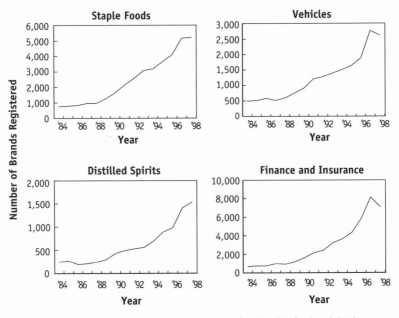

Figure 17-1 represents an analysis that evaluates the total number of new brands in four large industries over a fifteen-year period (1984–1998). The data show an explosion in the number of new brands in each industry through the 1990s.

dustries has grown at a rate of 23.5 percent. Even in an undeniably mature category such as staple foods, trademarks have grown nearly seven times as fast as revenues. While the number of marks has skyrocketed in relation to revenue, marketing and promotion (M&P) support has lagged revenue growth. In some cases, as in autos, the relationship between mark growth and M&P support is nearly inverted.[4]

The number of brands and brand portfolios will continue to grow. Just as portfolios are becoming more complex, so too is managing them. Consider the sheer number of people involved in marketing a brand these days. To take just one slice of an example, consider a distribution channel partner—say the bar owner selling Anheuser-Busch beer. In the 1990s, Anheuser-Busch made a conscious decision to avoid Swedish Bikini Team-esque imagery in favor of a two-track creative plan of running gags and product quality messages. But they still must work with the bar owners asking for promotional funds to sponsor wet tee-shirt contests.

To follow that line of thinking for a moment, partners can also influence a brand in less well-intended ways. Gillette made a big impact with the introduction of its three-bladed Mach3 shaving system in 1998. Then, in 1999, CVS—one of Gillette's major retail partners—rolled out its own private-label Acti-Flexx three-blade razor. It now hangs next to Gillette's revolutionary product at anywhere between $1 and $2 less.

Even invisible partners like suppliers can affect brands. Consider the case of Anita Roddick and The Body Shop. Roddick founded her business as a single store in the United Kingdom in 1976 and grew it into the most maverick of institutions and, arguably, the most holistic of brands. She eschewed questionable third world labor practices, animal testing, and toxic ingredients in her line of health and beauty products. "We simply and honestly sell wholesome products that women want," she said. "We sell them at reasonable prices without exploiting anyone, without hurting animals, without hurting the earth. We do it without lying, cheating and without even advertising."

The company was stunned in 1994, when *Business Ethics* magazine called into question some of its earth-friendly claims.

In a series of articles by investigative reporter Jon Entine, the magazine published some startling revelations about the ingredients with which the company made its soft-spoken products. Entine revealed that, in addition to the organic ingredients Roddick traveled the world to find and trade for, other Body Shop product ingredients included nonrenewable petrochemicals and substances lab-tested on animals. The reporter also discovered that some batches of products had come out contaminated and containing formaldehyde. Any number of media outlets picked up on the story, including eco-friendly National Public Radio, battering the company over the course of two years.[5]

Net/net, brand portfolio management is not going to get any simpler. The solution? We think it is to invest in building the organizational capability around brand portfolio management. Create molecules. Replace the infrastructure. Invest in better information systems. Get ahead of the curve.

Keys to Success

As consultants, we are sometimes tossed out of a CEO's office, not because she doesn't buy what we're saying, but because we've said it ten different times in ten different ways, and will go for eleven, given a chance. Therefore we do not want to belabor the challenges of organizational resistance. *But* ... (Here we go again.) But brand portfolio management is going to take some big changes, and the best way to make it work is to make sure all the pieces are in place beforehand.

- Use the molecule to get everyone to the same place in terms of definition. The Molecule should Rule.
- Lock in the change program by driving the change top-down.
- Put the infrastructure in place to allow the change to happen.

18 | lessons learned in the trenches

Some problems are so complex that you have to be highly intelligent and well informed just to be undecided about them.
—Laurence J. Peter, *Peter's Almanac*

NOW YOU KNOW what we know. Almost. You now understand the theory and current practice of brand portfolio management and you have the frameworks with which to put this knowledge to use. But there is also a set of more pragmatic lessons we have gleaned from working on problems under the real-life pressures of tight budgets, incomplete data sets, and organizational politics. We can't take credit for every case study we presented in the past seventeeen chapters, but we did watch, listen, and learn. What we picked up may be helpful as you get started. Here they are— our lessons learned.

Action/Reaction

Sir Isaac Newton first observed that for every action, there is an equal and opposite reaction: the Third Law of Motion. This law of action and reaction also holds for brand portfolios. Simply put,

Anything that will make a brand portfolio more attractive to one group will make it less attractive to another.

Nothing comes for free. Nabisco, in the 1990s, dutifully followed the consumer trends toward spicier foods with a series of extensions of its A1 Steak Sauce. As it rolled out the new products, it put its heaviest media focus on them. A1 Bold & Spicy and A1 Thick & Hearty, for example, took the bulk of A1 brand advertising during their launches. The company managed to score an impressive jump in shelf facings in stores. But by 1997, A1 managers realized, the focus on new flavor variations had siphoned the pull of the overall A1 brand. Although the trademark brown bottle and red-and-white label enjoyed tremendous consumer equity and a 39.4 percent share of the $232 million steak sauce category, Nabisco research found that in fact, consumers who kept the product in the fridge used it only rarely. Consumers didn't use A1 in 90 percent of all steaks consumed, the data revealed. And the extensions simply weren't performing up to expectations; sales of Bold & Spicy in particular dropped by 38.2 percent versus the previous year.

In its 1996 annual report, Nabisco offered shareholders a self-effacing apology along with a promise to put the core brand back on the front burner. In mid-1997, the company embarked on a broad but basic revamping of the line, pegged to the restaurant-industry revival of steakhouses. It set up an "A1 Rolling Steakhouse Tour," offering samples and free recipes in high-traffic events over thirty weeks in 1998 and saw its sales jump 5 percent in the sales period. It also redesigned the entire line, putting the extensions in packaging that conformed better to the core A1 bottle, thus creating a more uniform brand front across its store facings. For its restaurant trade customers, Nabisco developed a series of promotional alliances that included consumer promotions such as an A1 co-branded steak sandwich at Subway Sandwich Shops.[1] The refocus on the core was very successful.

Many attempts to reposition a brand or extend a brand portfolio encounter a wave of offsetting and usually unexpected reactions. Brand extensions, added to the portfolio to attract new customers, instead cannibalize existing volumes and add marketing costs. Attempts to broaden the overall portfolio positioning to provide a broader base for growth result in a diluted marketing message and require additions of new strategic brands to fill the void. Repositioning efforts intended to attract new customers leave existing customers behind. Agreements with marketing partners lead to fundamental changes in what the brand stands for. New products, intended to add luster to the overall brand portfolio, prove to be Edsels, fading quickly and taking some brand portfolio equity with them.

For example, it is easy in hindsight to deconstruct how the licensing ventures described in chapter 11 went awry. But in real time, as he negotiated and signed the deals, Calvin Klein did not foresee the potential flip-side result. Nor did Miller Brewing Company anticipate that Lite would draw most of its volume from the core Miller brand. Since the introduction of Miller Lite by the way, sales of Miller's regular beer brands have all declined substantially.[2] Fox Television has found that a series of gimmicky, exploitative shows such as *Who Wants to Marry a Millionaire?*, *When Animals Attack,* and *World's Worst Drivers* have sullied its image.[3]

These are all examples of cases where an action, well intended, created an unexpected adverse reaction. Of course sometimes, the unexpected reaction is positive. But we wouldn't count on luck to bail you out of poorly thought through strategies. The important idea is that there will be consequences to every strategy. Whenever an agency proposes a repositioning program or the new business department suggests a co-branding venture, it pays to spend time "what-iffing," setting up measures that will provide early warning of unwanted changes, and creating contingency plans. Brand portfolio managers must understand and anticipate inverse consequences every bit as much as they preach the potential benefits of their action plans.

Simplicity

Occam's Razor says:

All things being equal, the simplest answer is usually the best.

For brand portfolios, it clearly applies. As we have seen, brand portfolios are naturally complex, far more extensive than they might appear at first blush. Each brand links to other brands in the portfolio in at least four dimensions. Boundaries are poorly defined and effects of changes difficult to predict. In a five-brand portfolio, there are one hundred combinations and four hundred possible relationships. In a ten-brand portfolio, there are over three million permutations. The sheer complexity is overwhelming. In the face of all that complexity, simplicity is a good thing.

For new brand portfolios, simplicity often occurs as a function of forethought. Saturn was one of the most successful car launches in history. In two years, despite a relatively small dealer network and a modest advertising budget, Saturn became the tenth-largest car company in the United States. In planning the launch, its executives hotly debated one nagging question: whether Saturn should develop distinctive model names in the Japanese and American carmaker tradition—for example, Chevrolet Lumina, Cadillac Escalade, Oldsmobile Aurora, and—or simple model numbers, as do many European manufacturers. Hal Riney, the advertising star whose agency masterminded the launch, argued for the simpler model numbers and won. By managing a portfolio with fewer components, the argument went, Saturn could better focus its strategy and resources.[4] He was right.

For older portfolios, the move toward simplicity is more complicated—requiring a reallocation of resources, understanding and acceptance on the part of many managers, channel partners, and the like. Despite spending over half a billion dollars to establish individual carline brands such as Vigor, Integra, and Legend, Honda's Acura division took Saturn's route in 1995 and moved to a far more simple portfolio using only numbers and letters to supporting the overall Acura brand.

Sometimes the marketplace, or company structure, pushes an organization to move toward a portfolio design that is more complex than it need be. In cases like that, we invoke the first rule—action begets reaction. It's important to think through the consequence of what may seem like a perfectly logical, natural move.

Harley-Davidson did just that with the Buell brand. Buell is the performance cousin to the Harley-Davidson brand portfolio. Buell has always enjoyed close ties to Harley. The founders were Harley alumni, and Harley provided encouragement and resources to help them get started. Harley controlled 49 percent of the company since 1993, and in 1998 acquired most of Buell's remaining stock.[5] Given their shared history, Harley and Buell executives mulled cross-pollinating brands to leverage the Harley name. They wisely made the decision to leave the Buell brand portfolio as separate as possible from the outset. While Buell shares many of the signature traits of the Harley brand portfolio—American manufacture, high quality, even some shared technology, and a shared dealer network, the brands differ markedly in terms of styling and buyer base. In Harley's purview, the chrome-heavy retro look plays an integral role in the Harley brand portfolio. Accordingly, linking the two portfolios would create enormous complexity, far more than the complexity of managing two semi-distinct portfolios.

In such instances, the simpler the brand portfolio, the easier it is to manage.

Unity/Not Homogeneity

As the Miller Beer case showed, brands that are not managed as a portfolio can end up getting in each other's way in the marketplace. Well done, portfolio management should provide a counter to this. If you're thinking about different roles for different brands, you'll likely encourage experimentation. If you have risk control measures in place, you should feel more comfortable about taking risks. In a word, brand portfolio management is a creative function.

In building brand portfolios, we want unity of purpose and cohesiveness. We do not want homogeneity and, especially, we don't want *bland* homogeneity. Steve Shugan, a marketing professor at the University of Chicago, tells his students, "Some people like hot tea, and some like iced tea, but no one likes lukewarm tea." It is up to all of us to make sure that thinking like a strategist does not mean losing the ability to think like a marketer—be aggressive, entrepreneurial, and creative.

19

the implications of infinity

> *To see a World in a Grain of Sand,*
> *And a Heaven in a Wild Flower,*
> *Hold Infinity in the palm of your hand,*
> *And Eternity in an hour.*
> —William Blake, *"Auguries of Innocence"*

BUSINESS BOOK TITLES are no place for modesty. But at first blush, the title of this book, *The Infinite Asset*, may seem excessive. We don't think so. When we use the word infinite, we are trying to capture two of the dimensions that make brands unique as a competitive asset.

The first is that brands are almost timeless. As you drive the interstate from Chicago to Gary, you pass a huge set of silos on the side toward the lake. The mammoth dun-colored concrete buildings are crumbling and falling down. On the side of one is the painted the name of the previous owner, Falstaff beer. The Falstaff brand began in St. Louis over a hundred years ago and today is made under contract by Pabst. It has lasted through changing strategies and different owners and loss of its breweries. And even more important, it has ɯaɯed a loyal customer base, including Elvis Cole, the hero of Robert Crais's famous series of detective novels. The brand is still alive, even though the concrete silos are crumbling to dust.

Brands and the lore around them can last for a very long time. It has been decades since Winston claimed "It tastes good like a cigarette should" or since Burma Shave planted poetry on the shoulders of America's roadways ("Does your husband/ Rant and rave/Shoot the brute/Some Burma Shave.") But consumers haven't forgotten them. Even consumers who are far too young to have first-hand knowledge of those campaigns are familiar with them. And as Packard Bell demonstrated, this latent equity is always available to the clever and farsighted brand portfolio manager.

Brand portfolios are also infinite from another perspective. They provide extraordinary leverage to their owners. As we have seen in numerous examples in this book—Vicks, Post-it, Philips—brand portfolios provide opportunities for growth without megamillion-dollar investments in new plants, property, and equipment. There are many types of assets—hard assets such as cash, factories, distribution networks, and patents, soft assets such as core competencies and organizational learnings. All are important. But all can be copied or made obsolete by a new advance, say by a bigger, newer factory, or by hiring away key executives. Except brands.

The battles between Microsoft, Yahoo!, and Netscape over Internet territory are great examples of the advantages brands have over harder assets like technology. As the Internet has grown, so has the battle to own consumer access, the platform from which consumers head off to travel the Net. Two types of companies have competed for this right: vendors who provide software to access and search the net, and Web sites, which offer home pages or portals. Since these companies also offer advertising space and merchandising deals to e-retailers, whoever provides access for the most consumers stands to enjoy revenue streams beyond software sales or service fees. If you look at three of the most prominent of these competitors— Microsoft, Netscape, and Yahoo!—the pros and cons of competing on the basis of brand versus other types of assets come into focus.

Netscape

Netscape Communications, whatever its more recent woes, arguably created this era of Web branding that we see as soon as we boot up our Macs and PCs each day. Ironically, Netscape was undone by a failure to capitalize on its creation.

Jim Clark and Marc Andreessen were the masterminds behind a service so pervasive now that we rarely think twice about it: the Web browser. This first-of-its-kind technology introduced millions of people to the Internet, and in doing so created a revolution in retail branding and information services. Clark and Andreessen made this technology universally available as "freeware," which allowed anyone to learn how to surf and discover the Internet.

From its inception in 1994, as Mosaic Communications, Netscape became a company that grew through innovation and a unique technology.

Andreessen sowed the seeds in January 1993, when he posted a new type of software application, then called X Mosaic and Mac Mosaic, on the embryonic Internet. Developed as a prototype at the National Center for Supercomputing Applications (NCSA) at the University of Illinois, Mosaic actually worked like the Web itself. It acted in such a way as to pull together documents, Internet search tools, scientific data, and other files under a single framework of hypertext "pages," manipulated by a seven-option menu still familiar today: File, Navigate, Options, Annotate, Documents, Manuals, and Help. Mosaic introduced the document universal resource locator (URL) as a navigational guide. Mosaic also used hypertext references to other key sites.

Clark hooked up with Andreessen, and in April 1994 they set up Mosaic Communications, at that point able to boast more than one million copies of Mosaic in circulation.[1] The two understood the eventual winning revenue model well before most dot-com entrepreneurs: "There are ways to advertise on the Internet, and we think we know exactly how to pull it off," Andreessen said at the time. Clark prophetically claimed the Internet was the "real information superhighway, a commercial marketplace."[2]

The new Netscape company in December 1994 shipped its Navigator 1.0, the first secure open software system able to handle private information and transactions, ten times faster than other network browsers and capable of running across Windows, Mac, or X Windows. The server software also offered real security and first-ever online commercial services like online publishing, financial services, and interactive shopping.[3]

Netscape Navigator 1.1 debuted the next spring and continued to raise the bar; it was faster now and set up to show text first, then graphics or photos, so that users could begin reading while they waited for the graphics to load onto the screen. Navigator 1.1 also added special backgrounds, blinking text, and even crude animation. Netscape share went to 75 percent of all Internet users. In August 1995, when Netscape went public, the company was valued at $2.2 billion, a figure that would triple soon thereafter.

In September 1995, Netscape released Navigator 2.0 and Navigator Gold 2.0. Its offerings now included access to live online applications, support for streaming video and audio, fully integrated browsing, e-mail, newsgroups, chat and File Transfer Protocol (FTP) capabilities, digital IDs and state-of-the-art message encryption, digital signatures, live editing, and a whole set of developer-side improvements.[4] Netscape also signed a license with the then powerful Internet service provider (ISP) Prodigy for Navigator 2.0 as the basis for its own Internet browser.[5]

At this point, Clark and Andreessen had garnered Bill Gates's attention. Depending on the source, Netscape could claim anywhere from 75 percent to 85 percent of browser share. Internet Explorer was technologically inferior. Microsoft rushed Internet Explorer 1.0 to meet the release of Windows 95, and it showed.[6] Internet Explorer 1.0 was slower than Navigator, couldn't display many of the same complex 3-D backgrounds and advanced page elements as Navigator, and did not support all the standard Netscape extensions.

The next May, Netscape wrapped a year-long dominance of the browser market with another innovative version, 3.0. Building on its leading technology, the new Navigator included a "shared whiteboard." This enabled users to talk to each other over the Internet simply collaborating on a shared document, the first online equivalent of a long-distance phone call. Navigator also gave users a new technique for more secure transactions that relied on electronic certificates issued by the vendor. Netscape built its lead and attempted to hold it by using technology as a primary strategic weapon. As we will show, it didn't work.

Yahoo!

The biggest-spending advertisers in the United States have for decades fallen into some basic categories: automotive, packaged goods, fast food, soft drinks, and financial services. But as Christmas 1999 approached, casual TV viewers in the United States began noticing a massive influx of new brands buttressing their national TV programming, brands invariably bearing the suffix ".com."

MySimon.com offered price comparison services on a world of products, searching the cheapest prices at local retailers. CNET.com offered non-techno information on computers and software. Amazon.com now offered toys and a raft of gift categories in addition to its earlier product base of books and music. Gift.com offered an interface through which consumers might program and purchase just the right gift for family or friends. Autoweb.com offered interactive services to shop for and buy a vehicle. Pets.com offered pet-store products delivered to one's door, because, as its ads averred, "pets can't drive." E*TRADE and Ameritrade bombarded Americans with offers of easy-access riches by way of individual stock trading. ABC had sold about 25 percent of its Super Bowl broadcast inventory a month after Christmas to "dot-com" companies, including sole sponsorship of its half time show to E*TRADE in a $3.8 million deal.[7]

Even amid this flood of services, brands, and clever ad hooks rushing out at Americans, one of the original and still best-trafficked brands on the Web had quietly built the breadth of its services to offer nearly everything the new dot-coms did. But now, as then, it was still known as, simply, Yahoo!

In 1994, company founders David Filo and Jerry Yang converted a hobby of tracking areas of their and friends' interest on the Web into a customized database accessible to consumers, a means to make the sometimes daunting Internet more navigable for plainer folks. Yahoo!, reputedly, served as an acronym for "Yet Another Hierarchical Officious Oracle database," indicative of Filo and Yang's populistic attitudes. After a year or so, however, even as they expanded their search and categorization capabilities, Filo, Yang, and their team realized that theirs was a replicable technology with no substantial barriers to the entry of others. True to the test, where they once operated with the minor self-assurance of an innovation window of sixty days, plus or minus, today they find most of their updates on Lycos or AOL the next day.

With this prophetic insight, in late November 1995, Yahoo! sold 12 percent to a group of now Internet regulars that included Softbank, Reuters New Media, and Capital Group Ventures.[8] Yahoo!, an already profitable, low-overhead operation, didn't need the money to fund its operations; rather, according to Jeffrey Mallet, then vice president of business operations, "Yahoo! wanted to make sure the company had funds in place to begin marketing and exposing the brand outside the 'in-the-know' Internet community."[9]

With the infusion of public money in the second quarter of 1996, Karen Edwards, vice president of marketing, used a budget of "hundreds of thousands of dollars" to push the Yahoo! brand.[10] For a brief two weeks in mid-1996, she took a quirky, homespun campaign to the airwaves in three strategic markets—New York, Los Angeles, and San Francisco.[11] Edwards also pursued wacky grassroots programs that included a "Yahoo! for Barry Bonds" sign that flashed at 3Com Park in San Francisco, and getting the brand into consumers' hands via licensed products, from Ziff-Davis's *Yahoo! Internet Life* magazine (400,000 readers) to snowboards.[12] She also went the co-branding route, bartering the lure of online media exposure for cross-promotional efforts with Ben & Jerry's, Sega, Visa, and MCI.[13]

Let's consider this in context. Yahoo! set about painting itself as a basic consumer brand well before many consumers knew what "Yahoo!" was. One early ad depicted an old fisherman off in a wilderness cabin boosting his catch hyperbolically with lure information obtained on Yahoo!—cue the company's trademark "ya-hoooo" yodel. Such imagery went more toward creating a folksy, personable brand than any nuts-and-bolts product message, leading one business wag at the Association of National Advertisers (ANA) conference in 1997 to characterize Yahoo! as "a friendly roadside diner on the information superhighway."

In the process, the company has been careful to actively manage the brand portfolio. Brand is so primary at Yahoo.com that, according to Edwards, it is almost intuitive. Named a *Brandweek* Marketer of the Year in 1997, Edwards has shepherded the portfolio through both organic and acquisitive growth.

Yahoo! began to make some big purchases: Geocities, Rocketmail, and Broadcast.com. Geocities became Yahoo! Geocities nearly overnight, the new parent quickly folding user-generated tailoring applications of the online community site into My Yahoo. Yahoo! immediately washed the site with its style and content, spreading its person-to-person auctions, e-mail, and instant messaging services to all the Geocities users.[14] Rocketmail users similarly found their services enhanced as Yahoo.mail clients with the addition of a "spam" mailbox, to filter out e-mail detected to be generated by a mass mailing.

The company considered a quirky sub-brand for its finance site, "On The Money," but quickly rethought the move in context of the brand and redubbed it Yahoo! Finance. The brand portfolio now includes Yahoo! Mail, Yahoo! Shopping, Yahoo! Broadcast, Yahoo! Bill Pay, Yahoo! Sports, Yahoo! Geocities, Yahoo! Auto, Yahoo! Auctions, etc. The company also uses Y! as a sort of abbreviational sub-brand, for services such as Y! Messenger, Y! Mobile, and Y! Greetings. It has developed a kids-only site dubbed Yahooligans!, which reflects the core brand in look and function.

Edwards says, "We're telling people to check out Yahoo! Finance, Yahoo! Sports, Yahoo! Shopping, but it's all about everything you can get with us, networked, at *Yahoo!* . . . One of things you have to keep in mind is, the majority of people using our services *find* services through Yahoo!. Everything we're doing offline is to make people know why they should come here in the first place, which is for a lot of singular reasons but is more important as an aggregate. It's the overall brand that you're tuning into. It's like The WB, a network where you expect and are given a certain kind of programming no matter what night of the week it is. At the end of the day, we want Yahoo! to stand for all these different things."[15]

"The key for Yahoo! growth is brand, quality content, and distribution," Tim Koogle, chairman and CEO, has stressed to the press on more than one occasion, putting "brand" first every time.[16] Brand has made Yahoo! a coveted partner of other mainstream brands, and in 1999, it even scored the company cross-content deals with Sprint Wireless and Kmart's Bluelight.com. Yahoo! in early 2000 tallied up a massive usage increase year-to-year—some 465 million page views per day for December 1999, compared to an average of 167 million page views per day in December 1998.

Yahoo! makes an interesting contrast with Netscape. Both are of similar age, both came about because of a technological innovation. But they chose very different strategies—one opted for the technology treadmill, the other for branding—and they have ended up at very different places. Still, Yahoo! is a relatively simple use of brand portfolio management. Yes, Yahoo! relied on a strong brand, and it has used some of the tools we discussed in Part 2, notably extensions and amalgamation. But there is an even better example of the use of a brand portfolio to compete against technology: Microsoft.

Microsoft

Microsoft has always been less about technology and more about using the brand portfolio. Nowhere is that more evident than in its efforts to grow in net space. In December 1996, Bill Gates made a speech at Pearl Harbor in which he opened the door between Sun Microsystems' Java Internet language and his army of programmers, signifying Microsoft's imminent leap into the online world. Until that point, computers to Gates had been units on consumers' tables and networks in office buildings. But as of Pearl Harbor '96, already embattled for approaching software monopoly, Microsoft was dedicating itself to similar ubiquity in linking up all those networks and units.

Microsoft's strategy was to use its enormous brand portfolio to attract co-branding and alliance partners. To do this, Microsoft used two of its most powerful brands, Microsoft and Windows, to help its browser brand, Internet Explorer, and its ISP brand, msn.com, catch up. As table 19-1 illustrates, early on the strategy focused on closing the technology gap between Microsoft's browser and Netscape Navigator. In 1996, Gates stepped up the plan to encompass enterprise-oriented technology partnerships, a broad set of distribution agreements that focused on ISPs, traditional retailers, and computer and related hardware manufacturers.

Microsoft faced a chasm between its Internet Explorer and the market leader in basic functionality. Instead of trying to cover that space with an R&D long jump, the company opted for a series of expansive partnerships to develop a package functionally equivalent to Netscape Navigator and compatible with programmers and users alike. Microsoft developed relationships with the two most prevalent applications at the time, the first with Sun Microsystems covering the use of its Java Internet application, touted at the time as the Internet's killer app."[17] Then Microsoft contracted with Oracle to license Visual Basic Script for inclusion in its Macintosh- and Windows-compatible browser products.[18]

To add substance to its browser functionality, the company inked a license with Spyglass Mosaic for use of its browser technology and World Wide Web publishing tool.[19] And a deal with Progressive Networks gave it use of the RealAudio player, and later its Personal Server; both became standard features of Microsoft's Internet Explorer.[20]

With the technology in place, and at least competitive functionality, Microsoft went after scores of ISPs in the United States and abroad, the biggest portals on the Internet, emerging technology manufacturers (e.g., WebTV, DirectTV), several cable operators, and even nontraditional channels for software (including USWeb[21] and Wal-Mart[22]). The list is a Who's Who of Internet access: the biggest ISPs in Mindspring,[23] Netcom,[24] Earthlink,[25] BellAtlantic,[26] and Ameritech,[27] and the biggest portals in AOL,[28] CompuServe,[29] and Prodigy.[30]

Through its license partnerships and a series of marketing and co-branding relationships, Microsoft brands became integral assets across any number of hardware and software products, as, for example, an added-value product add-on with a computer purchase, or using a compatibility license to endorse

TABLE 19-1

Microsoft Technology Alliances

	1995	1996	1997	1998
Technology	Progressive	UUNET	Intervista	ArborText
	Network	Blue Sky	Matrox	DataChannel
	Real Audio	Software	PenOp	Inso
	InContext	Motorola	Hewlett-	
	Spider	Citrix	Packard	
	Spyglass	Colusa	Verifone	
	Browser	Software	Alladin	
	Sun Micro-	Dolby Labs	Systems	
	systems	Intel DEC	Navitel	
	Java	NTN Comm.	Apple	
	Oracle VBS	FTP Software		
	IBM	Metrowerks		
	Netscape	Adobe		
		Macromedia		
		QUALCOMM		
		White Pine		
		Software		
		Dimension X		
		Verisign		
		Cyberion		
		Net Objects		
		Everex		
		Software		
		TrueVision		
		PointCast		

Table 19-1 identifies companies with whom Microsoft signed technology partnerships between 1995 and 1998. The companies listed announced agreements in the popular press during the corresponding year.

We reviewed the Microsoft company profile found on DJI (http://www.djinteractive.com) in order to compile the information listed in table 19-1.

another company's software product. Consumers, in other words, browsed software shelves looking for the "Windows-compatible" stamps. In 1997, Microsoft inked a broadened set of distribution agreements, this time in the cable industry, and a comprehensive set of content licenses.

Most would expect that Microsoft would be able to tie up a number of substantive agreements among a set of technology companies, but just as impressive was the company's use of brand alliances to boost customer acquisition. In the telecommunications industry, Microsoft signed up MCI, AT&T, Sprint,[31] British Telephone,[32] France Telecom and Deutsche Telekom AG,[33] and six of the seven Baby Bells[34] from the outset of its alliance strategy in 1996. The first deal, with MCI, set the stage for the rest, including collaboration on Internet and online ventures, cross-selling to MCI customers, and substantial cross-marketing efforts.[35] Microsoft even worked with MCI and DEC to address intranet applications.[36]

The alliances continued. With ConferTech, Microsoft jointly developed and marketed desktop audio, data, and video conferencing services.[37] Microsoft worked with Yahoo! to create an Autosearch feature, making Web searches on that engine faster and more efficient for users of Internet.[38] With StarSight, Microsoft made inroads on the development of interactive TV.[39] Each of these relationships provided an engine for long-term future growth opportunities.

The last piece of the alliance puzzle, one that Gates saw as a key area of differentiation, involved actual content offerings on the Internet Explorer start page, thus making it a destination unto itself. See table 19-2 for a partial list of the content-related alliances Microsoft struck in 1996 and 1997. Internet Explorer used a number of "channels," designated locations on the Web for users interested in a certain topic. For a content provider, such as MTVOnline or WSJ.com (the *Wall Street Journal* online), a designation as an Internet Explorer channel was obviously prime real estate. As with the other efforts, Microsoft spared no ambition in its target partners, signing up MTV for music news and features, ESPN for sports, Dow Jones and Dunn & Bradstreet for financial information, Microwarehouse for technological information (and shopping), Time Warner for entertainment, and the Mayo Clinic for health information services. These relationships gave Internet Explorer a real advantage in terms of users' perception of Microsoft as an interface with other prime brand portfolios, and the deals locked those brands out as potential assets for competitors, forcing them to align with less trafficked, less well-known channels on their software.[40]

In all, Microsoft established 127 alliances and co-branding relationships. Only by using the powerful Microsoft and Windows brands could it attract the partners it wanted and bootstrap its newer brands. By using its brand portfolio, it quickly ramped up its portal business in a way not possible by any other means. Microsoft created value in the space between brands.

TABLE 19-2

Microsoft Content Alliances

1996	1997
ESPNET Sports Zone	Headland Digital
Hollywood Online	Media (Pearson)
MTVOnline	Reed Elsevier
InvestorsEdge	Dunn and Bradstreet
MicroWarehouse	First Call
Riddler.com	Forbes
WSJ Interactive	Time Warner
	Dow Jones
	TVNZ One News
	Intuit (Quicken)
	IVI Publishing (Mayo Clinic)
	Wave Phone
	Greenhouse Networks
	Data Channel
	Audio Net
	Wired Digital

Table 19-2 identifies companies with whom Microsoft signed content-sharing partnerships in 1996 and 1997. The companies listed announced agreements in the popular press during the corresponding year.

We reviewed the Microsoft company profile found on DJI (http://www.djinteractive.com) in order to compile the information listed in table 19-2.

And as we finish this chapter, they're at it again, this time taking aim at the emerging wireless market. Microsoft and Starbucks are teaming up to provide wireless Internet access in Starbucks stores designed for "paying subscribers of Microsoft's Internet service," who eventually will use a Starbucks card to pay. Another company, MobileStar Network, is providing the complementary wireless data network, which will form the backbone of the operation.[41]

Head-to-Head

As Netscape's case attests, technology proved to be a less-powerful advantage than brand. By August 1996, for all the territory Netscape had pioneered, Microsoft had moved to eliminate Navigator's unique points of difference. In that month, Microsoft shipped Explorer 3.0, considered by many to be Navigator's equal from a performance and technological standpoint. For all of Netscape's inroads and firsts, it found itself losing out to Microsoft's bigger, stronger, better-deployed brand portfolio.[42] For example, Internet Explorer came free with PCs or Microsoft bundled it into its own hot-selling Windows software. Netscape complained to the FTC, but it was too late. The momentum had shifted.[43]

As of October 1996, Netscape's valuation had declined by 57 percent, to $3 billion, in nine months. Second-quarter sales were $75 million, but profits only $906,000, a disparity due solely to the huge development requirements for forthcoming new products. *Fortune* ran an article under the headline "Contemplating Netscape's Funeral."[44] Over the six months to follow, Internet Explorer usage would grow an average of 310 percent, while Navigator usage would decline 160 percent.[45] In March 1997, Jupiter Communications' Consumer Internet Technologies Group put Navigator's market share at 59 percent and forecast a drop to 38 percent by the end of the year. Internet Explorer's market share stood at 21 percent.

In May 1997, Netscape unveiled another attempt to combat the Microsoft brand portfolio and its alliances: a beta version of Netscape Communicator. Netscape positioned Communicator as an open-standards browsing, e-mail, and groupware service. But both Microsoft and Lotus, tapping IBM's considerable business client base, had already met the needs of intra-networked clients with fully Web-integrated and time-tested products for e-mail and network software. Their broader suites precluded the need for even the advanced Netscape product.

When, in September 1997, *PC Magazine* evaluated Microsoft Internet Explorer 4.0 and Netscape Communicator 4.0 in a performance face-off, Microsoft won.[46] A little more than a year later, Microsoft had assumed the lead in market share, at 44 percent to Netscape's 41 percent. In October 1998, AOL purchased Netscape for $4.2 billion in stock. Notwithstanding this deal, AOL CEO Steve Case, it was revealed, wanted to keep Internet Explorer as a component of AOL's ubiquitous software...in exchange for prime placement on the Windows startup desktop.[47]

Yahoo! won because it quickly realized that technology was not likely to be sustainable, that it needed to base its business on a more sustainable competitive asset, brand. Microsoft won ultimately, not by being first or most distinct, but by leveraging a portfolio. Yahoo! proved brand is more powerful than technology. Microsoft proved "brands," with an *s* is more powerful than "brand." For Clark and Andreessen, reliance on technology *alone* proved fatal, specifically because it occurred in a period and an industry in which technology can be so easily replicated.

A Final Thought

If you're driving a lonely country road with three hungry preschoolers in the back seat, branding is not very important. If the only restaurant in sight is a McDonald's, that's good. But if the only restaurant in sight is Harry's House of Hash and Haberdashery, and if the noise from the back seat is loud enough, you're stopping. The McDonald's brand doesn't bring much in a noncompetitive world.

But in a world with a McDonald's on the right side of the road and a Burger King across the street, the McDonald's name suddenly becomes valuable. And on a strip with a Burger King, a Wendy's, a Carl Jr.'s, and a dozen others, suddenly the Mc-Donald's brand becomes worth gold—especially if the Happy Meal prize is a character from the kids' favorite movie or TV show. In the final event, that's why brands are so important. The more intense the competition, the more valuable the brand in relative terms.

To actually release this value requires understanding how to manage not just a brand, but brands. The true value is being created in the spaces between brands, in combining brands in new ways, and in creating portfolios of brands with extraordinary strength and competitive flexibility. The possibilities are infinite.

afterword: about the research

We are suffering from a plethora of surmise, conjecture and hypothesis. The difficulty is to separate the framework of fact— of absolute undeniable fact—from the embellishments of theorists and reporters.
—Sherlock Holmes *in* Arthur Conan Doyle,
   "Silver Blaze"

THE FRAMEWORK AND toolkit we presented in this book grew out of four types of research. First, our consulting work—thirty years' worth between the two of us. Our clients offer a good cross section of the marketing world, spanning consumer and B2B enterprises, companies that sell products and companies that sell services, and those that operate in both established and high-tech categories. Where possible, we have referred to these clients by name.

Second, new case studies. We developed four case studies specifically for this book: Cadillac, Miller Beer, 3M, and one on the broader "Portal Wars," using Yahoo! as a primary example. Cadillac, we believe, is unfortunately a great example of a company that is mismanaging its brand portfolio. Miller Beer offers an extraordinary example of the failure of one of the world's most sophisticated marketers to perpetuate and grow a successful brand, despite having the single most successful new product introduction of the postwar era. On the other hand, 3M illustrates marketing best practice. An industrial company from Minneapolis may seem an unusual place to find a structured approach to brand portfolio management that might just serve as a model for future brand managers, but there it is. Finally, Yahoo! and its use of the brand portfolio as a competitive weapon provide cogent lessons that also transfer easily from the virtual world to bricks and mortar.

Third, select cases from earlier work. Specifically, we updated our case studies on Harley-Davidson, Apple Computer, Providian, Iams, and Boston Beer, and we used those companies extensively as examples of good and bad brand portfolio management.

And fourth, the popular press and academic literature. As you've seen, we have drawn examples from those sources to enhance our descriptions of certain theories, good behaviors, and bad practices, and to supplement our own illustrations.

On the process side, we have invested almost two years in analyzing brands and brand portfolios. We started out by testing the hypothesis that the brand set is indeed growing at a much larger rate than ever before. That work began at the U.S. Patent and Trademark Office, which tracks U.S. trademarks and servicemarks via a database called CASSIS, or the Classification and Search Support Information System. CASSIS divvies its data into ten specific industry classifications (SICs) and contains over one million individual data points. Converting these data into usable proxies for brands required considerable processing. "Ford Company license plate frames" for example, has a trademark distinct from Ford Company. After a great deal of manual processing, we created a clean and usable data set.

For the purposes of our analysis, we looked at four broad industry classifications: the motor vehicles industry (including literally anything with a motor), the wine and spirits industry, the staple foods industry (including frozen foods, grocery, dairy, and meat, poultry, and fish), and the financial services industry (which includes insurance services). In combination, these four industries account for roughly 22 percent of all domestic consumption and over 15 percent of U.S. Gross Domestic Product. They provide a reasonably broad view across a range of industry types, from consumer to B2B, services to goods, hard goods to soft.

After working through the database to ensure consistency and eliminate duplications, we ended up with a robust and deep data set of brands and would-be brands covering an extended time period. With this data set, we created the brand trend analyses used in chapters 1, 6, and 17.

We also analyzed thirty companies (listed on the left in table AW-1), putting particular emphasis on thirteen portfolios.

For each portfolio, we considered the total number of brands in the portfolio, ranked each one according to its importance in the consumer purchasing decision and its influence on the portfolio as a whole, and then calculated a series of normative ratios that we could use to describe the portfolio quantitatively. These ratios include size, relative interconnection to other portfolios, and degree of control, among others. For each subsystem, we evaluated not only the number of brands present and their relative importance to the portfolio, but also how and where the portfolio connected with other brand portfolios. For example, consider how the McDonald's portfolio is closely tied to Disney's through a long-standing series of marketing and promotional efforts. We also analyzed how each brand in the portfolio related to the others. The most straightforward way to describe our analyses is to compare them to those plastic molecules we all constructed long ago in chemistry class. In this case, though, the molecules were very large, and since we had no elemental table to rely on, we had to create every atom particle by particle.

In the interest of full disclosure, we have labeled our work with the portfolios on the list "illustrative." Most brand portfolios have a large library of market research data accumulated over years of analysis. The best way to build molecules is to use these data. However, we had access to only a portion of these libraries. And we would not have used confidential proprietary data in this book, even if we had all these data. Instead we worked with secondary, publicly available information to create

TABLE AW-1

Companies and Portfolios Analyzed

Companies	Portfolios
American Express	Green Card
America Online (AOL)	
Anheuseur-Busch	Budweiser
Apple	iMac
Booz·Allen & Hamilton	
Callaway Golf	
Charles Schwab	
DaimlerChrysler	
EMC	
Ford	
General Motors (GM)	Cadillac
Gillette	Mach3
Harley-Davidson	
Intel	Pentium
Karsten	PING
Kodak	
Lego	
Levi Strauss	
Microsoft	Windows
Miller Beer	
Morgan Stanley Dean Witter	Van Kampen
Nestlé	Crunch
Netscape	Communicator
Nike	
Pepsi	
PricewaterhouseCoopers (PwC)	
Procter & Gamble (P&G)	Pantene
Starbucks	Frappuccino
3M	
Young & Rubicam	

We have studied the brand set within each of the thirty corporations listed in table AW-1. The companies span technology, consumer package goods, consumer hard goods, business-to-business manufacturers, automotive, financial services, and consumer manufacturing industries. For each corporation we inventoried their brands and classified them under our methodology. We mapped the specific brand portfolios for the thirteen corporations listed in the right-hand column.

the molecules. These analyses are used throughout the book, but are most critical to chapters 3, 4, 5, and 14.

Some of the ideas and solutions we floated in this book have been successfully implemented, some have been implemented and the results are pending, and some have been only partially implemented but are very promising. All of them, however, have their roots in the real world.

We have aimed to give you, our readers, not only some new and hopefully provocative thinking about brand portfolio management, but also to provide tangible take-away, in the form of an approach to valuing and leveraging your brand portfolio at a level you had previously not thought possible. What's more, we have tried to render simple what is in fact an enormously complex topic. But as Justice Oliver Wendell Holmes said, "I would not give a fig for the simplicity this side of complexity, but I would give my life for the simplicity on the other side of complexity." We didn't, in other words, try to be simple for simple's sake. Our intent was to provide a robust and helpful approach to creating value using brand portfolios.

We think we've done just that. We hope you agree.

acknowledgments

I set out one summer on an island off the coast of Scotland to write a splendid book, one that people would remember forever. It has taken far longer than ever I expected.
  —J. P. Donleavy, preface to the Penguin Edition
  of *The Ginger Man*

We set out to write a book that would simplify the task of managing complex brand portfolios. And, like J. P. Donleavy, it has taken far longer than we ever expected. Therefore, our first thanks must go to our long-suffering agent, Philip Spitzer, and our editor, Kirsten Sandberg. On the topic of Kirsten, she has reshaped this book at every level—fundamental ideas, story line, and wording—and now it is a much better book than we could have created on our own. Also at HBS Press, we thank Jill Connor, Erin Korey, and Walter Keichel.

Our thanks also go to the many other people who contributed to the writing of this book. For the first draft, Matthew Grimm, former editor of *Brandweek*, signed on to help turn our consultingese into readable prose. As it turned out, he did far more than that, challenging ideas and providing case studies. Regina Fazio Maruca filled a similar role on the final draft. Jamison Wong, Jana Volavka, Katie Deutsch, Jed Freedlander, Akhil Gupta, and Jane Megquier all helped with research. Randy Johnson figured out how to create a 3-D brand molecule, and did so after two other design firms had walked away shaking their heads.

We also thank our clients and colleagues for input and suggestions. Peter Georgescu of Y&R and Ben Shapiro of Harvard were particularly helpful at the early stages, when our draft was so bad it had to be deciphered instead of read. Dean Adams and Anne Greer of 3M; Joan A. Goldsmith; Don Schultz and Phillip Kotler of Northwestern University; Ruth Mills and Andrew Jaffee of John Wiley; John Sviokla of Diamond Technology Partners; Kathy Button Bell, CMO of Emerson; Stewart Owen of Y&R; Tom O'Toole, VP of Marketing at Hyatt; Ken Lambert; David Newkirk of Booz•Allen & Hamilton; Marcel Belt of Reckitt-Benckisser; Paul Hemp of the *Harvard Business Review*; and Steve Silver all contributed insightful comments.

Robin Wolfson, Danny Stern, Tom Neilsen, and Larry Leeson, of Leigh Speakers Bureau; Tom Miller of the Master's Forum; Dan Goldstein of the Direct Marketing Association; Greg Mather of the Northwestern Corporation; Kenneth Neher of SmithKline Beecham; Tom Woodside of Bath and Body Works; Jeff Negrin of ThompsonConnect; John Horton; and others provided fresh eyes, and their feedback was invaluable in refining the work.

The anonymous reviewers provided clear direction, which hopefully we have followed. We thank them all for their generosity of time and for their encouragement.

Speaking of encouragement, there is another group we need to thank for talking us down off the ledge when it seemed the book would never get written: Barbara Martz, Brian Fischer, Joel Kurtzman, Jack Lederer, and Michael A. Hill. It is unbelievably lonely when the second draft isn't working and you are already nine months late. Small kindnesses mean more than you know.

And finally, all of our clients ask great questions, but several asked them in such a way that we had to write this book to answer them. Special thanks to: Ed Kaplan, CEO, and Jack LeVann, former executive vice president of strategy at Zebra Technologies, Mike Childers of Northwestern Corporation, Barry Asin of Adecco, Brian Dickie of TXU, and Giovanna Imperia of Compaq.

notes

Chapter 1

1. Philip Kotler, *Marketing Management* (Prentice Hall, 1991), 482.
2. Steve Liesman and Carla Anne Robbins, "Forum Sues Harvard, Two Ex-Advisers," *Wall Street Journal,* 25 October 2000.
3. This is still not a sound example of effective umbrella branding. See Part 2.
4. David Aaker, *Building Strong Brands* (Free Press, 1996), 242.
5. Kevin Lane Keller, *Strategic Brand Management* (Prentice Hall, 1998), 392.
6. Jay Tolson, "What's in a Name? When it's a Brand, Lots, Including Image, Money, Power," *US News and World Report,* 9 October 2000, 52.

Chapter 2

1. Iams has since been purchased by Procter & Gamble.
2. Most managers and analysts will probably use computer simulation to create the brand molecule, as we did, which allows far more subtle grading than simply black, white, or gray.
3. Kevin Lane Keller, *Strategic Brand Management* (Prentice Hall, 1998), 375–376.

4. Robert Johnson, "Cutthroat Business: How Universal Makes a Killing at Halloween," *Wall Street Journal*, 31 October 2000.

5. IQ Section (*Adweek Interactive Report*), "Dot-Bombs," *Adweek*, 27 November 2000, 17.

6. David Kiley, "Pontiac Pumps $100M Into Grand Am In Biggest Model Push," *Brandweek*, 25 May 1998, 8.

7. Becky Ebenkamp, "We're All Brands Around Here," Superbrands Section, *Brandweek*, 21 June 1999, S13.

8. Starbucks employee, interview by Sam Hill, 42nd St. and Madison Ave. New York City, 24 November 1999.

Chapter 3

1. Jacob Jacoby, George Szybillo, and Jacqueline Busato-Schach, "Information Acquisition Behavior in Brand Choice Situations," *Journal of Consumer Research*, no. 3 (1977): 212.

2. Automotive News Market Data Book, quoted by Rick Popely in the *Chicago Tribune*, "The New Look of Luxury Imports and SUV's Take Over the High End for Bummer Car Buyers," 5 November 2000.

3. Brand management is a commonly used term. In practice, actual implementation varies widely among companies. For example, compare 3M's very different interpretation in chapter 16.

4. David Aaker, *Building Strong Brands* (Free Press, 1996), 242.

5. There are several alternative approaches to this. One is to create a set of positioning axes based on the market research for each set of brands. For example, perhaps it is possible to map the Cadillac system using the axes of Luxury, Performance, and Value. Or "Currency" (defined as up-to-date image). We have not yet debugged any of the alternative approaches.

Chapter 4

1. This visualization works well for services, industrials, and consumer durables. It's less useful for consumer package goods.

2. "Record 1999 Sales," *Car & Truck News*, 28 February 2000.

3. Jerry Ball, "Too Cool for Chrysler?" *Wall Street Journal*, 20 July 2000, B1.

4. Glen Sandford, "1985-1993," <http://www.apple history.com/h4.html> (accessed 20 July 2000).

5. Joe Wilcox, "New Mac Cravings Leave Some Buyers Hungry," 4 August 2000, <http://www.news.cnet.com/news/0-1006-200-2435027.html?tag=st.ne.1006.sndstry.ni> (accessed 11 August 2000).

6. Lucas Graves, "1999 Marketers of the Year: Apple Computer," *Marketing Computers*, January 1999, <http://www.marketingcomputers.com/mc/search/article_display.jsp?vnu_content_id=427070> (accessed 11 August 2000).

7. Dennis Sellers, "Apple Sales up 25 Percent Overall," *MacCentral*, 22 December 1999, <http://www.maccentral.com/macworld.com/news/9912/22.salesup.shtml> (accessed 11 August 2000).

8. Graves, "1999 Marketers of the Year: Apple Computer."

9. Ball, "Too Cool for Chrysler?"

10. iMac now works with other ISPs as well.

Chapter 5

1. Credit Suisse/First Boston.

2. Tim Tresslar, "Iams: A year after the sale," *Dayton Daily News*, 6 August 2000.

3. Microsoft is a particularly unwieldy system. There were over 600 registered trademarks for the company in 1999. We have noted only those that were unique and live.

Chapter 6

1. This is debatable. In the late 1980s, the U.K. consultancy Interbrand had begun valuing brands as stand-alone entities to enable companies to reflect them more accurately on their balance sheets.

2. David Aaker, *Managing Brand Equity* (Free Press, 1991), 17.

3. Tony Jackson, "In a Grey Area," *Financial Times*, 6 December 1996.

4. Richard Cole, "Odwalla Says Recall is Complete," *Seattle Times*, 2 November 1996.

5. Gregory L. White, and Joseph B. White, "GM Is Likely to Phase Out Oldsmobile," *Wall Street Journal*, 12 December 2000; and Vanessa O'Connell and Joseph B. White, "After Decades of Brand Bodywork, GM Parks Oldsmobile—For Good," *Wall Street Journal*, 13 December 2000.

6. As we write this, there is some speculation that it was actually problems with Ford's recommended tire pressures that created these problems, and thus it could be argued that Ford contaminated the Firestone system. Either way, the point stands.

Chapter 7

1. Peter H. Farquhar et al., "Strategies for Leveraging Master Brands: How to Bypass the Risks of Direct Extension," *Marketing Research*, no. 4 (1992): 32.
2. Al Ries and Laura Ries, *The 22 Immutable Laws of Branding* (HarperCollins, 1998), 11.
3. Betsey Spethmann, "Big Talk, Little Dollars," *Brandweek*, 23 January 1995 on front cover, continued to page 6.
4. Jean B. Romeo, "The Effect of Negative Information on the Evaluations of Brand Extensions and the Family Brand," *Advances in Consumer Research*, no. 18 (1991): 399.
5. Jim Mateja, "Cadillac's New Mid-Size Catera Is Everything Cimarron Was Not," *Ft. Lauderdale Sun-Sentinel*, 9 December 1996.
6. Pam Weisz, "Tartars Set To Do Battle," *Adweek East/National*, 28 March 1994, 9; "Arm & Hammer sets sights on Mentadent," Client News, *Adweek East/National*, 27 June 1994, 13; John McManus, ed., "SuperBrands 97 Category Ranking: Health & Beauty Aids," SuperBrands Section, *Brandweek*, October 1996; Matt Grimm, ed., "SuperBrands 96 Category Ranking: Health & Beauty Aids," SuperBrands Section, *Brandweek*, November 1995.
7. Carolyn Dunn, "The Oral Care Market," Household and Personal Products on the Internet," February 1998, <http://www.happi.com /special/feb981.htm> (accessed 9 March 2001).
8. James Hickey, "The Oral Care Market," Household and Personal Products on the Internet," February 2000, <http://www.happi.com/special/feb002.htm> (accessed 9 March 2001).
9. Charlotte Mason and George Milne, "An Approach for Identifying Cannibalization within Product Line Extensions and Multi-Line Strategies," *Journal of Business Research*, no. 31 (1994): 163–170.

10. This is the next frontier for this vein of research. As more portfolios are mapped and their performance compared, these sorts of heuristics should become more established.

11. Motoko Rich, "Holiday Inn Express Aims to Hone Image," *Wall Street Journal*, 24 July 2000.

12. Barbara Loken, Deborah Roedder John, "Diluting Brand Beliefs: When do Brand Extensions have a Negative Effect?" *Journal of Marketing*, no. 57 (1993): 3.

13. Thomas K. Grose, "Brand New Goods," *Time*, 1 November 1999, 110.

Chapter 8

1. Jean-Noel Kapferer, *Strategic Brand Management: Creating and Sustaining Brand Equity Long Term* (Free Press, 1992), 96.

2. Based on calculation of shares of top thirty brands representing 43 percent of the market. Helios calculation based on data from *Global Drinks Records*, Euromoney Publications, 1999.

3. Kevin Lane Keller, *Strategic Brand Management: Building, Managing and Measuring Brand Equity* (Prentice Hall, 1998), 116.

4. Xerox even thought of moving to "The Knowledge Company" at one point.

5. Don Sexton, "Branding" (speech given at the DuPont Internal Branding Forum, Wilmington, Delaware, 16 September 1999) and subsequent follow-up telephone conversation with Sam Hill, 27 July 2000. Given the dearth of good case studies of repositionings, the authors have urged Dr. Sexton to publish this excellent example.

6. Michael R. Riley, "Joseph Schlitz Brewing Co.: A Chronological History," 28 January 2001, <http://www.antiquibles.com /schlitz/history.htm>.

Chapter 9

1. Johnson & Johnson, Australia, under the leadership of Fred Vermeer and Chris Kelly.

2. T. R. Knudsen et al., "Current Research: Brand Consolidation Makes a Lot of Economic Sense," *McKinsey Quarterly*, no. 4 (1997): 189–193.

3. Ernest Beck, "Still Hungry, Unilever Faces Full Plate Now," *Wall Street Journal*, 31 May 2000.

4. A *Los Angeles Times* article, "Briefly/Consumer Products: Unilever's Acquisitions Boost Profit," (5 August 2000, C2) suggests Unilever does not see a difference between cutting brands and reducing support levels.

5. Vanessa O'Connell and Joseph B. White, "After Decades of Brand Bodywork, GM Parks Oldsmobile—For Good," *Wall Street Journal*, 13 December 2000.

6. John O.Whitney, "Strategic Renewal for Business Units," *Harvard Business Review*, July–August 1996, 85.

7. Associated Press Wire, "Massive Brand Reduction Planned to Save $1.4 Billion," *Chicago Tribune*, 22 September 1999.

8. Emily Nelson and Nikhil Deogun, "Course Correction: Reformer Jager Was Too Much for P&G; So What Will Work?—Under New Boss Lafley, Firm Still Has a Need to Get Its Sales Growth Moving—Another Earnings Warning," *Wall Street Journal*, 9 June 2000, A1.

9. Whitney, "Strategic Renewal for Business Units."

10. "P&G sells Clearasil to UK Chain," *Plain Dealer* (Cleveland, OH), 18 October 2000.

11. "Dial to Acquire the Coast Brand From Procter & Gamble," *PR Newswire*, 25 April 2000.

12. Laurie Flynn, "Packard Bell Striking Pay Dirt with Consumer-Market Strategy," *San Diego Union Tribune*, 22 November 1994.

Chapter 10

1. Christina Binkley, "Marriott Aims New Brand at Families, Women Travelers," *Wall Street Journal*, 13 October 1998.

2. John J. Keller, "Maw Bell: AT&T Lays Plans to Gobble Local Phone Service," *Wall Street Journal*, 21 August 1995, A4.

3. Earle Eldridge, "AutoNation Changes Gears, Car Seller Plans to put Local Names on its Dealerships," *USA Today*, 13 July 2000.

4. Ibid. The irony is that in this example, Florida's Maroone franchise was originally owned (and therefore sold to AutoNation) by Michael E. Maroone, the current Chief Operating Officer of AutoNation.

5. Amy Barrett, "Gucci's Big Makeover Is Turning Heads," *Wall Street Journal*, 26 August 1997.

6. "Pegasus Launches New Corporate Identity Strategy," *PR Newswire*, 22 February 1999 <http://www.pegsinc.com>.

Chapter 11

1. Almar Latour, "Portable Technology Takes the Next Step: Electronics You Can Wear," *Wall Street Journal*, 19 August 2000.
2. Thomas K. Grose, "Brand New Goods," *Time*, 1 Novebmer 1999, 100. The exact statistic is for licensing, but in that licensing was the most prevalent form of brand alliance at the time, it seems safe to extend the observation to all alliances.
3. A. R. Rao and Robert Ruekert, "Brand Alliances as Signals of Product Quality," *Sloan Management Review*, no. 36 (1994): 87.
4. Daniel C. Smith, "The Effects of Brand Portfolio Characteristics on Consumer Evaluations of Brand Extensions," *Journal of Marketing Research*, no. 131n2 (1994): 229. The specific discussion was in the context of extensions whose quality was at odds with that of the overall portfolio.
5. Clare Sambrook, "Do Free Flights Really Build Brands?" *Marketing* (UK), 15 October 1992, 11.
6. Teri Agins and Rebecca Quick, "Behind a Bitter Lawsuit by Calvin Klein Lies Grit of Licensing," *Wall Street Journal*, 31 May 2000, and "Calvin Klein is Suing Maker of Its Jeans," *Wall Street Journal*, 1 June 2000.
7. Agins and Quick, "Calvin Klein is Suing Maker of Its Jeans."
8. Rao and Ruekert, "Brand Alliances as Signals of Product Quality."
9. Theresa Howard, "McDonald's Continues Search on Job That Some See as Devalued Lately," *Brandweek*, 12 October 1998, 43.

Chapter 12

1. Alexei Barrionuevo, "British Petroleum Plans to Remodel Its Gas Stations," *Wall Street Journal*, 25 July 2000.
2. "Media Metrix Releases the Top 50 At Home and Business Digital Media Web Sites," *Business Wire*, 20 January 2000.
3. Ernest Beck, "Unilever Renames Cleanser, Tidying Its Brand Portfolio," *Wall Street Journal*, 27 December 2000.

4. "Global Corporate Report—Corporate Focus: Nestlé Won't Crunch Its Brands—Food Giant Points to Re-organization," *Wall Street Journal Europe,* 24 September 1999.

5. William Glanz, "Name Change Costly for New Banks Owner," *Washington Times* (Washington, D.C), 26 April 1999.

6. Exhibit in the lobby of PricewaterhouseCoopers' world headquarters.

7. James Surowieki, "You Name It: When Corporate Big Shots Should Leave Well Enough Alone," *Slate,* 12 July 1997, <http://www.slate.msn.com/motleyfool/97-07-11/motleyfool/asp> (accessed 9 March 2001).

8. "Sierra Inc. Introduces New Brand Strategy," *Business Wire,* 18 May 1998.

Chapter 13

1. Bloomberg News, "HP, Agilent Shares Soar," *Seattle Times,* 18 November 1999, E4.

2. Jon Fortt, "Life in the Spin-Off Lane: Employees Can Undergo a Kind of Separation Anxiety when Firms like 3Com and Palm Part Ways," *San Jose Mercury News,* 24 July 2000.

3. <http://www.hp.com> (accessed 10 March 2000).

4. "HP Reports Third Quarter Results," 16 August, 2000, <http:// www.hp.com/financials/quarters/2000/q3.html> (accessed on 28 July 2000).

5. Zeneca itself was a recent spin-off from ICI.

6. Susan Scherreik, "Ferreting Out Stealth Spin-Offs: These Offerings Tend to Fall Through the Cracks," *Business Week,* 13 December 1999, 196.

7. Ken Brown, "Andersen Consulting Becomes Accenture," *Wall Street Journal,* 27 October 2000, B6.

8. Beth Berselli, "Retooling at Black & Decker; In a Return to Core Products, the Home Appliance Line Will Go," *Washington Post,* 9 February 1998, 10.

9. Greg Farrell, "Dockers Sees Younger Men in Nice Pants," *USA Today,* 13 September 1999.

10. Sam Zuckerman, "Providian to Return Millions/No Wrongdoing Acknowledged," *San Francisco Chronicle,* 29 June 2000, B1.

11. For some, like GE, which spans everything from finance to small appliances to jet engines, it was probably a long time ago.

12. "North American Business Brief: Black & Decker," *Wall Street Journal Europe,* 22 June 1994, 10.

Chapter 14

1. <http://www.hoovers.com/hoov/about/index.html> (accessed 3 November 2000).
2. Shelly Branch, "Vodka on the Rocks," *Wall Street Journal,* 21 December 2000.
3. <http://www.hoovers.com/hoov/about/index.html> (accessed 3 November 2000).
4. Clayton Christensen, "Innovator's Dilemma," (speech given to the 16th Annual International Telecom Management Forum, Venice, Italy, 7 June 1999).
5. Mark Maynard, "Power to the People: Honda Accord Gets a V-6," *San Diego Union-Tribune,* 31 December 1994.
6. <http://www.hoovers.com/hoov/about/index.html> (accessed 3 November 2000).
7. <http://www.rolex.com> (accessed 19 March 2001).
8. Judith Rehak, "Exclusive Watches: When Time is Money U.S. Market for High-End Timepieces Grows," *International Herald Tribune,* 18 December 1999, 15.
9. Ibid.
10. Branch, "Vodka on the Rocks," A1.
11. Sam Hill and Glenn Rifkin, *Radical Marketing* (HarperCollins, 1998), 257.

Chapter 15

1. See Aaker, *Building Strong Brands,* chapter 10, for a richer discussion of the various levels of brand success.
2. Based on our research of publicly available data.
3. A great engineer. Both authors own PING equipment and realize that without Mr. Solheim's brilliance, we would never have finished this book, because we would still be in the woods off the seventeenth fairway looking for our balls.
4. Gerry Khermouch and Cathy Taylor, "Christening a New Flagship," *Brandweek,* 27 November 1995 on front cover, continued to page 6.
5. Trevor Jensen, "Miller Beer Gets Additional Help," *Adweek/National,* 20 May 1996, 68.

6. Gerry Khermouch, "Miller: Focus Off Miller Beer, on Lite" *Brandweek*, 30 September 1996, 4.

7. Shelly Garcia, "Red Dog Is About to Lose His Bite," *Adweek/National*, 10 June 1996, 52; media figures per Competitive Media Reporting.

8. "CDNOW, Interscope Geffen A&M Records and Miller Launch Innovative Custom CD Promotion," 27 July 1999, *PR Newswire*, Dow Jones Interactive.

9. Laurie Russo, "Takin' It to the Streets," *Beverage World*, 15 November 2000, 64.

Chapter 16

1. Scott Miller, "Revving Up Ford's Luxury Marques," *Wall Street Journal*, 10 July 2000.

2. In 3M terminology, this is brand management. As we note in chapter 17, in practice the definition of brand management varies widely across companies. We believe most companies think of brand management using the package goods definition of "one brand, one manager." What 3M calls brand management does not meet this definition and is, in practice, very close to what we term brand portfolio management.

3. Form 10-K, U.S. Securities and Exchange Commission, December 1999.

4. 3M Managers, telephone conversation with authors, 10 November 1999.

5. 3M Managers, interviews with authors, Minneapolis, MN, 31 March 2000 and 23 June 2000.

6. Again, every organization has its own vocabulary. 3M calls Post-it Software Notes, Post-it Easel Pads, and Post-it Flags products, but by our definition they are brands, just small ones.

7. This is not just an organizational exercise. It is critical that managers create the brand portfolio vision and guidelines before they are ever needed. This may seem a bit pedantic, but the number of choices is so large, the time exigencies so pressing and the trade-offs so complex that, unless clear rules are laid out *in advance*, it will prove difficult or impossible to make the right call when the time comes. When Lorillard Tobacco approached Harley-Davidson about a Harley cigarette in 1986, Harley's active licensing execs signed on the dotted line. It seemed like a good idea at the time. It wasn't. Fearing its

broad-based brand allure might help make cigarettes appeal to children, and with the number of liability suits against tobacco companies are on the rise, Harley second guessed itself almost immediately and began fighting to nullify the deal. But the mistake is understandable. In business, as in life, many decisions that make sense in the moment seem less sensible later.

Chapter 17

1. Jennifer Kent, "Brands Grow like Weeds on the Shelves of Grocers," *Rocky Mountain News* (Denver, CO), 1 July 1993, 62a.
2. Jeff Harrington, "Lagging Brands a Challenge for Firms Like Procter & Gamble," Gannett News Service, 25 August 1994.
3. Lois Therrien, "Brands on the Run," *Business Week*, 9 April 1993, 26.
4. Helios proprietary research.
5. John Stauber and Sheldon Rampton, *Toxic Sludge Is Good For You* (Common Courage Press, 1995), 74, and Charles P. Wallace with Ed Brown, "Can the Body Shop Shape Up?" *Fortune*, 15 April 1996, 119.

Chapter 18

1. Stephanie Thompson, "A-list: Nabisco's A1 Gets Multi-Pronged Revamp," *Brandweek*, 14 July 1997, 6.
2. Al Reis and Laura Reis, "Checking the Brandbook," *Brandweek*, 9 November 1998, 49.
3. Joe Flint, "This Reality Show Could Be Called: Who Wants to Be a Philanderer?" *Wall Street Journal*, 3 January 2001.
4. Hill and Rifkin, *Radical Marketing*, 258.
5. Associated Press Newswires, "Harley-Davidson Acquires Buell Motorcycle Co.," 21 February 1998, <http://www.ptg.djnr.com/ccroot/asp/publib/story.asp> (accessed 15 March 2001).

Chapter 19

1. John Markof, "New Venture in Cyberspace by Silicon Graphics Founder," *New York Times Abstracts*, 7 May 1994.
2. Tim Clark, "Making Money off Mosaic, Silicon Graphics' Clark Forms Company to Market Internet Software,"

Advertising Age, 16 May 1994, 22.

3. "Netscape Communications Ships Release 1.0 of Netscape Navigator and Netsite Servers, " *PR Newswire,* 15 December 1994, <http://www.proto.netscape.com/newsref/pr/newsrelease8.html> (accessed 18 March 2001).

4. "NETSCAPE: Introducing Netscape Navigator 2.0 and Netscape Navigator Gold 2.0," *M2 Presswire,* 19 September 1995.

5. Michael Moeller, "Prodigy, CompuServe to Broaden Net Reach," *PC Week,* 18 September 1995, 1.

6. Scott Arpajian, "Microsoft Ramps the Net," *Windows Sources,* 1 December 1995, 40.

7. Terry Lefton, "E*Trading Up," *Brandweek,* 22 November 1999, 65.

8. David Einstein, "Big Guns Backing Internet's Yahoo!" *San Francisco Chronicle,* 29 November 1995.

9. Ibid.

10. "Yahoo! Reports Second Quarter Financial Results," *PR Newswire,* 10 July 1996, and Jeffrey M. O'Brien, "Behind the Yahoo!" *Brandweek,* 28 June 1999, 17.

11. *Seattle Times* News Services, "Personal Technology Net News: Yahoo! Turns to TV Ads for Name Recognition," *Seattle Times,* 28 April 1996, C2.

12. Patricia Nakache, "Secrets of the New Brand Builders: AOL, Yahoo!, Palm Computing—a few innovative Infotech stars have built powerhouse consumer brands in little time. You may be able to follow their lead," *Fortune,* 22 June 1998, 167ff.

13. Information Access Company, "Sega Committed to Extending Yahoo! Brand to Consumer Products," *Multimedia Entertainment & Technology Report,* 26 September 1997.

14. Tish Williams, "Yahoo! Gets Personal," *UPSIDE Today,* 28 January 1999.

15. Karen Edwards, telephone conversation with Chris Lederer and Matthew Grimm, September 1999.

16. Yahoo! CEO Presentation at Paine Webber Internet Conference, 14 April 1997. NBC Professional Transcripts.

17. Fran Gardner, "Jiving with JAVA," *Portland Oregonian,* 8 December 1995.

18. "Microsoft Joins the Game, Firm Reveals Internet Strategy—Embrace and Extend the Net," *Internet Week,* 11 December 1995.

19. Howard Wolinsky, "Microsoft Moves Benefit Spyglass," *Chicago Sun-Times*, 8 December 1995; "Microsoft, InContext Do Web Authoring Deal," Newsbytes News Network, 20 November 1995; "Microsoft Introduces Browser," *Internet Week*, 21 August 1995.

20. "Progressive Networks and Microsoft Announce Streaming Media Agreement," *Business Wire*, 12 March 1996.

21. "Microsoft and USWeb Form Strategic Alliance to Help Businesses Take Advantage of the Web," *PR Newswire*, 11 December 1996.

22. The Associated Press, "Microsoft Signs Deals with MCI, Wal-Mart," *News Tribune* (Tacoma, WA), 30 January 1996.

23. "Microsoft, Mindspring Announce Agreement," *Business Wire*, 17 September 1996.

24. "Netcom Licenses Microsoft Internet Explorer; The Complete Internet Services Provider Broadens Alliance With Microsoft," *PR Newswire*, 12 March 1996.

25. "Earthlink: Microsoft and Earthlink Network Announce a Joint Partnership Agreement," *M2 Presswire*, 30 September1996.

26. "Newsline: Bell Atlantic, BellSouth Each Announce Internet Access Plans," *Multimedia & Videodisc Monitor* (Future Systems, Inc.), 1 May 1996.

27. "Ameritech Teams with Microsoft to Give Consumers Faster, Easier Way to Obtain ISDN," *Telephone IP News*, 1 April 1996.

28. "AOL Alliances Imply Revenue Shift," *Interactive Content*, 1 March 1996.

29. "Compuserve Licenses Microsoft's Internet Explorer Browser," *Media Daily*, 7 December 1995.

30. "Prodigy/ Microsoft: Prodigy To Use ActiveX Technology," *Dow Jones News Service*, 8 October 1996.

31. "Sprint Internet Passport Expands Reach With Release To The General Public," *Business Wire*, 4 December 1996.

32. Eric Reguly, "Business BT and Microsoft in Joint Venture," *The Times of London*, 5 July 1996, 26.

33. "Microsoft To Market Digital Lines With Europe Cos.," Capital Markets Report, *Wall Street Journal*, 26 September 1996.

34. "Microsoft Makes Alliances to Quicken Internet Access," *Orlando Sentinel*, 10 March 1996, A18.

35. "MCI Jilts News Corp. for Microsoft," *Interactive Content*, 1 January 1996.

36. Audrey Choi and Don Clark, "MCI and Digital to Join Microsoft in Intranet Deal; Alliance Expected to Challenge AT&T in Corporate Data Networks," *The Globe and Mail,* 8 April 1996.

37. "Confertech and Microsoft Sign Agreement on Joint Development and Marketing Efforts," *PR Newswire,* 28 May 1996.

38. "Microsoft and Yahoo! Make Web Searches Easier For Microsoft Internet Explorer 3.0 Users," *PR Newswire,* 13 August 1996.

39. "Microsoft Invests $20 Million in StarSight Telecast," *Multimedia Week,* 26 August 1996.

40. "Major Content Providers Team with Microsoft to Attract Users," *New Media Week,* 19 August 1996.

41. Rebecca Buckman, "Starbucks Joins Microsoft to Serve Web With Its Coffee," *Wall Street Journal,* 4 January 2001.

42. "Looking for the Sweet Spot: Netscape Takes on Microsoft," *Software Futures,* 1 October 1996.

43. Kim S. Nash, "Explorer Beta Gains Ground on Navigator," *ComputerWorld,* 22 July 1996, 1a.

44. Stewart Alsop and Alicia Moore, "Contemplating Netscape's Funeral," *Fortune,* 30 September 1996, 213+.

45. "MICROSOFT: It's Official ... Microsoft Internet Explorer 3.0 is the Fastest Growing Browser," *M2 Presswire,* 7 February 1997.

46. *PC Magazine* Experts Available to Discuss Microsoft Internet Explorer 4.0 Release," *PR Newswire,* 30 September 1997.

47. Jared Sandberg, "NET GAIN America Online's bold deal with Netscape is a high-stakes gamble on the Internet, e-commerce and how technology will affect your life," *Newsweek,* 7 December 1998, 46–49.

index

about the authors

Sam Hill

As president of Helios Consulting, Sam Hill works with very senior executives on the topics of growth strategy, marketing, and brands. In its second full year, Helios reached revenues of $2.5 million. It has a staff of ten, offices in New York and Chicago, and a client list that includes Young & Rubicam, TXU, Compaq, eGM, Alcoa, Brigg's & Stratton, Zebra Technologies, and HarperCollins.

Sam spends his time working with clients, writing, and speaking. His work has appeared in *Strategy & Business, Estrategia & Negocios, The Financial Times,* and the *Wall Street Journal,* and has been featured in *Business 2.O,* the *Harvard Business Review, Salon,* and the *New York Times.* In 2001, his occasional commentaries for *Fortune Small Business* magazine will become a column. Sam's first book, *Radical Marketing,* co-written with Glenn Rifkin and published in 1998, is now in its fifth printing and is being translated into seven languages. It was named one of Fortune's Best Business Books of 1999. In a typical year, he speaks to some ten thousand executives at twenty-five major forums in seven countries.

Before cofounding Helios, Sam was vice chairman and chief strategic officer in New York at D'Arcy, the world's twelfth largest advertising agency, and chief marketing officer and lead partner at Booz•Allen & Hamilton in Chicago and Sydney, Australia. He began his career at Kraft General Foods as an engineer and later served as director of international strategy. He has a degree in engineering from the University of Georgia and an M.B.A. from the University of Chicago. He lives with his wife and teenage children in Winnetka, Illinois.

Chris Lederer

Chris Lederer, a cofounder Helios Consulting, spends most of his time consulting to very senior marketing and management executives on the issues of brand strategy and growth strategy. Chris's particular areas of expertise are optimizing complex brand portfolios and e-branding. His work in this area has appeared in the *Harvard Business Review.*

Before cofounding Helios, Chris held significant positions at Booz•Allen & Hamilton, Lever Brothers, North Castle Partner Advertising, and RJR/Nabisco. He is a board member at ecompanystore.com and El Click.com. Chris has an M.B.A. from Columbia Business School and a B.S. in economics from Washington and Lee, where he was recognized as a Robert E. Lee scholar. He lives in Manhattan with his wife and their two young daughters.

For more information, please visit the Helios Web site: *www.heliosconsulting.com.*